America
at Random
Q&A

America at Random Q&A

Jerome Agel

PRIAM BOOKS
ARBOR HOUSE
NEW YORK

Questions

1 ▪ "Fellow citizens, we cannot escape history. We...will be remembered in spite of ourselves" was vouchsafed by

    (a) Thomas Jefferson.
    (b) Abraham Lincoln.
    (c) H. L. Mencken.
    (d) Walter Lippmann.

_____ 1

2 ▪ Two aliens have been voted honorary citizenship by Congress:

    (a) Winston Churchill and Raoul Wallenberg.
    (b) Marie Curie and Albert Schweitzer.
    (c) Winston Churchill and the Marquis de Lafayette.
    (d) Lawrence of Arabia and Mahatma Gandhi.

_____ 2

3 ▪ Benjamin Franklin (1706–1790) proposed that the Great Seal, "the Representative of Our Country," show

    (a) Pharaoh engulfed by the waters of the Red Sea while pursuing the children of Israel.
    (b) a rattlesnake and the slogan Don't Tread on Me!
    (c) an eagle.
    (d) the _Mayflower_.

_____ 3

ANSWERS ON PAGE 175 ▪

ANSWERS ON PAGE 175

4 ▪ Paul Revere (1735–1818), who never made it to Concord or to Lexington that night in '75,

    (a) became a spy for the British and lived out his life near London.

    (b) announced that the Revolution was not his cup of tea (taxed or otherwise) and retired to his silversmithing.

    (c) led a disastrous raid on the British at Penobscot, Maine, and was court-martialed.

    (d) married the widow of George Washington, in 1803.

_____ **4**

5 ▪ After political collisions with Congress led to impeachment proceedings, and after deciding not to seek the Republicans' nomination for the presidency in 1868, President Andrew Johnson

    (a) won a seat in Congress.

    (b) threw thirty shekels into the well of the House of Representatives and hanged himself.

    (c) tried with Jefferson Davis to resurrect the Confederacy.

    (d) became "the national drunkard," fulfilling a promise to drink a gallon of "likker" in every state whose representatives had voted against him in his congressional trial.

_____ **5**

6 ▪ Four "conspirators" were hanged following a street demon-
stration demanding

    (a) the resignation of President Abraham Lincoln.
    (b) a reduction of the ten–hour work day, six days a week,
        to eight hours per day.
    (c) the U.S. pull out of the Great War in their native Europe.
    (d) the pope cancel his plans to visit the U.S.

_____ **6**

ANSWERS ON PAGE 176 ▪

7 ▪ Wealthy Boston patriot John Hancock, first to put his name to the Declaration of Independence and twice a president of the Continental Congress,

   (a) decided that he couldn't afford to work in government and started an insurance company.
   (b) lectured throughout the thirteen states and leaked tavern gossip everywhere about the Founding Fathers.
   (c) ran four times for the presidency, losing out to George Washington (twice), Thomas Jefferson and James Monroe.
   (d) was an inept treasurer of Harvard College (1773–1777) for four years.

_____ 7

8 ▪ George Washington (1732–1799) was appointed by Congress to the grade of General of the Armies of the United States in

   (a) 1776.
   (b) 1779.
   (c) 1786.
   (d) 1976.

_____ 8

9 ▪ _____tried to have the inscription "In God We Trust" removed from U.S. coins.

   (a) Theodore Roosevelt
   (b) Norman Thomas
   (c) Earl Warren
   (d) Francis Joseph Spellman

_____ 9

10 ▪ Igor Fëdorovich Stravinsky (1882–1971) became an American citizen in the early 1940s and presently found himself in hot water with police.

    (a) He had composed and conducted his own version of "The Star-spangled Banner."

    (b) His *Rite of Spring* was considered "too sexy by far" by Boston's flying blue squad.

    (c) He refused to marry his mistress of seventeen years, invoking the "Maxim Gorky maxim."

    (d) He made speeches critical of his native Russia, at the time a U.S. ally in the Second World War.

_____ **10**

11 ▪ Thomas Jefferson's epitaph "Here was buried Thomas Jefferson, author of the Declaration of Independence, of the Statute of Virginia for Religious Freedom, and father of the University of Virginia"—was composed by

    (a) John Adams.

    (b) Washington Irving.

    (c) Jefferson himself.

    (d) Anonymous.

_____ **11**

12 ▪ One of the most famous photographs in American history shows a midget sitting on a fat knee of millionaire J. P. Morgan, Jr. (1867–1943). A circus press agent's stunt, the photograph—made in 1933 while the stern-faced Morgan was waiting to testify before a Senate banking and currency committee—unintentionally turned Morgan into a benign old dodderer. The twenty-seven-inch-tall midget, a plump, well-proportioned brunette named Lya Graf,

(a) appeared on the cover of the first issue of *Life* magazine.
(b) was killed in Auschwitz.
(c) was given a million dollars by the House of Morgan.
(d) refused to do her circus act until her salary was quadrupled.

_____ **12**

13 ▪ President Abraham Lincoln (1809–1865) cast around for a way out of slavery and struck upon a stunning compromise.

(a) Everyone in the country would be considered to be a slave; then it would be every man for himself.
(b) The black slaves would work half a year for their white masters and the masters would then work half a year for their slaves—doing identical work.
(c) The slaves would be freed right away and their owners paid off with a large loan floated for the purpose.
(d) The slaves would be put into the army, and those who survived basic training would be given their freedom at the end of the thirteen-week period.

_____ **13**

14 ▪ "The right of citizens of the United States, who are eighteen years of age or older, to vote shall not be denied or abridged by the United States or by any State on account of age." The Twenty-sixth Amendment was ratified in

(a) 1857.
(b) 1911.
(c) 1971.
(d) 1981.

———— **14**

15 ▪ When the Founding Fathers drafted and promulgated the Declaration of Independence, the Liberty Bell was

(a) not rung.
(b) cracked and could be rung only one time, which it was.
(c) rung every thirteen seconds for thirteen consecutive days and nights.
(d) out of town—having been borrowed by the villages of Concord and Lexington for display at a local fair.

———— **15**

16 ▪ William Kemmler was the first American to be

(a) awarded the Nobel Prize in astrophysics.
(b) honored by the Tchaikovsky Piano Scholarship Committee in Moscow.
(c) executed by electrocution.
(d) a star player on a Wales cricket team, which, incidentally, went on to win the Empire Games in Auckland, New Zealand, in 1926.

———— **16**

17 ▪ Until_____was president, Jews could not hold public office in Maryland.

    (a) William Howard Taft
    (b) John Quincy Adams
    (c) William Henry Harrison
    (d) Benjamin Harrison

_____ **17**

18 ▪ Not until_____did the last three of the fourteen states in the Union, at the time that the first ten amendments to the Constitution were drawn, ratify the amendments—the Bill of Rights.

    (a) 1797
    (b) 1823
    (c) 1885
    (d) 1941

_____ **18**

19 ▪ Irving Berlin (1888–   ) wrote "God Bless America" for

    (a) the twenty-first birthday party of Alice Roosevelt, President Theodore Roosevelt's rambunctious daughter.
    (b) the tenth anniversary of Armistice Day.
    (c) a girlie show.
    (d) a tribute to Jesse Owens' spectacular track and field victories in the Summer Olympics in Berlin in 1936.

_____ **19**

20 ▪ Declaring it a "covenant with death and an agreement with hell...a compromise with tyranny," the abolitionist William Lloyd Garrison (1805–1879) burned a copy of_____ at a public ceremony near Boston on the Fourth of July 1854.

(a) the Declaration of Independence
(b) the Monroe Doctrine
(c) the Magna Charta
(d) the Constitution

_____ **20**

21 ▪ When the first American representative to China, John E. Ward, entered Peking in 1859,

(a) an angry impasse ensued.
(b) he obsequiously kowtowed.
(c) he was asked to strangle a coolie to prove that he believed in the rule of the Dowager Princess.
(d) he had to lie about Commodore Perry's historic voyage to Japan earlier in the decade.

_____ **21**

22 ▪ Five of his relatives served the Confederate cause:

(a) Abraham Lincoln.
(b) Ulysses S. Grant.
(c) John Brown.
(d) Dred Scott.

_____ **22**

23 ▪ The name the White House became official when

    (a) the architect Stanford White drew up plans for renovation.

    (b) President Theodore Roosevelt had it engraved upon his stationery.

    (c) the mansion was restored after the War of 1812.

    (d) Congress approved its construction during President George Washington's second term.

_____ **23**

24 ▪ Peter Minuit, best known for having bought Manhattan for a song, was relieved as director general of New Netherlands five years later

    (a) for having conned the Indians.

    (b) when he wrote pornography, the first in the New World.

    (c) for shady dealings with Dutch Reformed ministers.

    (d) when the West India Company learned that he could have bought the island for six dollars worth of beads instead of the twenty-four dollars he paid.

_____ **24**

25 ▪ Between the second president, John Adams, and the twenty-seventh president, Woodrow Wilson, no president

    (a) received more than 50 percent of the popular vote.

    (b) made an appearance before Congress.

    (c) was married in the White House.

    (d) declared war against another country.

_____ **25**

26 ▪ Nearly a century before the *Mayflower* weighed anchor off Cape Cod in 1620

    (a) the mainland coast of the Gulf of California was already an outpost of New Spain.

    (b) Pilgrims from France had settled around New York Bay.

    (c) Indians were sailing east across the Great Ocean Sea and "discovering" the Old World.

    (d) another *Mayflower* from England and Holland had reached Hawaii.

_____ **26**

27 ▪ He played baseball in an army camp in Cooperstown, New York, in 1839, and suddenly there was a legend, still hotly debated, that Abner Doubleday (1819–1893) had created out of the game one old cat the modern version of the national pastime. (The teams fielded eleven players.) We *do* know for sure that Doubleday

    (a) was hailed for his contributions to the sporting life in America and took over the coaching of all athletic teams at West Point, from which he had been graduated, in 1842.

    (b) invented football.

    (c) founded an important publishing empire, with offices in New York and most European and Asian capitals.

    (d) fired back the first Union gun in defense of Fort Sumter, in Charleston Bay, in the first armed contest in the Civil War in April 1861.

_____ **27**

28 ▪ The social reformer Jane Addams (1860–1935), denounced as a traitor and the "most dangerous woman in America,"

    (a) married Bernard Shaw, and together they terrorized the consciences of Europe and America.

    (b) chose suicide as the only way to escape the slanderous charges.

    (c) turned over her Hull House in Chicago to Father Flanagan of Boys Town.

    (d) was awarded the Nobel Peace Prize.

_____ **28**

29 ▪ Twice, _____ was asked by President Abraham Lincoln to be a Union general and head a Union army in the Civil War and twice he turned him down.

    (a) Robert E. Lee

    (b) Giuseppe Garibaldi

    (c) George Washington's great-great grandson Thomas

    (d) Charles Cornwallis

_____ **29**

30 ▪ The Philadelphia seamstress Elizabeth Griscom Ross didn't design and sew the original flag of the United States, but she was celebrated at the time for

    (a) spying for the British on the proceedings in Independence Hall.

    (b) making the colors for Pennsylvania state ships.

    (c) balancing a two-year romance with both Benjamin Franklin (by day) and John Hancock (by night).

    (d) serving as recording secretary of both the First and Second Continental Congresses.

_____ **30**

31 ▪ Friendly, shy John Thomas Scopes (1901–1970), teacher of general science and coach of athletics, became in 1925 the focus of the historic freedom-of-speech "monkey trial" when he answered an appeal by the American Civil Liberties Union for someone willing to challenge the new Tennessee law forbidding the teaching of Darwin's theory of evolution in contradistinction to the biblical interpretation of man's creation. The jury's verdict:

(a) guilty.
(b) Scopes and his lawyer, Clarence Darrow, must spend the rest of their lives in a cage with "another pair of baboons."
(c) not guilty.
(d) Scopes must read the Bible aloud, cover to cover, in a Tennessee church.

_____ 31

32 ▪ The Pony Express was a galloping success for

(a) seventy-one years until Wells Fargo let it go out of business.
(b) more than one hundred fifty years.
(c) less than two years.
(d) for exactly half a century, minus exactly one day.

_____ 32

33 ▪ The first and only congressman to be jailed for criticizing the president,_____was reelected while serving four months behind bars and emerged a national hero.

(a) Robert LaFollette
(b) Alger Hiss
(c) Aaron Burr
(d) Matthew Lyon

_____ 33

34 ▪ Less than a decade after that historic December 17 of 1903 at Kitty Hawk, North Carolina, Wilbur Wright

(a) was mysteriously struck dumb for the rest of his life.
(b) died of typhoid.
(c) flew non-stop from Washington, D.C., to Chicago.
(d) had a falling out with his brother, Orville, and set up his own bicycle shop, in Tulsa.

_____ 34

35 ▪ The Cherokee Sequoyah is the only man in recorded history

(a) to win a prize for chemistry and a prize for photography in the same year.
(b) to conceive from the resources of his own mind and perfect in its entirety an alphabet, or syllabary.
(c) to swim the Pacific Ocean from Japan to Oregon.
(d) to learn how the pyramids were built (only to have his papers and drawings destroyed in an accidental fire a few days after his death).

_____ 35

36 ▪ Before Congress decided that the responsibility was the nation's and not an individual's,_____personally paid pensions to widows of former presidents.

    (a) Babe Ruth
    (b) William S. Paley
    (c) Andrew Carnegie
    (d) Oliver Wendell Holmes, Jr.

_____ **36**

37 ▪ A former mayor of New Orleans, Nicholas Girod (1747– 1840), had a breathtaking plan:

    (a) pluck the exiled Napoleon from a dot of land in the South Atlantic and set him up in Louisiana.
    (b) make the city the vice capital of the world—*that* would solve its tax problems.
    (c) turn the city over to blacks and make it off limits to whites.
    (d) secede from both the Union and the Confederacy, change the name of the city to Jacksonville (in honor of General Andrew Jackson, who had whipped the British in the Battle of New Orleans, in 1815), and make Jacksonville a nation unto itself.

_____ **37**

21

38 ▪ Before he uttered the memorable question, "Dr. Livingstone, I presume?," the journalist-explorer Henry Morton Stanley (1841–1904)

(a) had found a tribe of Amazon women.

(b) had fought for both the Union and the Confederacy in the Civil War.

(c) had sailed three times around the world, never once going ashore in nearly six years.

(d) had improved the cotton gin to the point that human hands were no longer needed in processing this most important of the vegetable fibers.

_____ **38**

39 ▪ When he was awarded a Pulitzer Prize for his novel *Arrowsmith*, Sinclair "Red" Lewis

(a) published a copy of the prize's text on the back page of every newspaper (daily and weekly) in the whole country.

(b) rejected the honor, saying that such prizes make writers "safe, obedient, and sterile."

(c) revealed that the book had been a team effort—five of his students at Williams had contributed a minimum of two chapters each, so what did prize committees know?

(d) confessed that he had copied it almost word for word from a manuscript that his mother had finished shortly before her death.

_____ **39**

40 ▪ Confederate General in Chief Robert E. Lee's father

    (a) was a Revolutionary War hero.
    (b) fought side by side with his son in the Civil War.
    (c) fought against his son in the Civil War.
    (d) was a confederate of Aaron Burr in the secession plot in the early 1800s.

_____ **40**

41 ▪ In a court trial Joseph Henry (1797–1878) was able to prove that

    (a) Mary Lincoln was indeed insane.
    (b) General Ulysses S. Grant could have ended the Civil War at least fifteen months earlier.
    (c) he, and not Samuel F. B. Morse, had invented the electromagnetic telegraph.
    (d) the large rocks that had fallen in Connecticut were not from outer space but had been dropped intentionally by a mischievous passing balloonist.

_____ **41**

23

■ ANSWERS ON PAGE 184

42 ▪ When he campaigned in 1848 to become the nation's twelfth president, "Rough and Ready"_____had never voted in a presidential election, had been in the army for four decades, was a slaveholder and was well known for being a sure-shot spitter with tobacco juice. He had also been a hero in the Mexican War, directing aboard his horse "Old Whitey" the capture of Monterrey in 1846, and vanquishing Mexican President Santa Anna's army of 20,000 at Buena Vista in 1847. He gained the Whig nomination over Henry Clay, Daniel Webster and General Winfield Scott, and at the polls licked the Democrat Lewis Cass and former President Martin Van Buren:

(a) Millard Fillmore
(b) William Henry Harrison
(c) Zachary Taylor
(d) James Buchanan

_____ **42**

43 ▪ After the anarchist Leon Czolgosz (1873–1901), with a revolver concealed in a handkerchief, had shot down President William McKinley (1843–1901) in a reception line, _____ was arrested when the assassin said that he had been influenced by her speeches and writings.

(a) Dorothy Day
(b) Carry Nation
(c) Emma Goldman
(d) Louella Parsons

_____ **43**

44 ▪ To protest_____, John Quincy Adams (1767–1848) wrote, "Myself an affectionate child of our alma mater, I would not be present to witness her disgrace in conferring her highest literary honors upon a barbarian who could not write a sentence of grammar and hardly could spell his own name."

(a) his mother's financial support of Herman Melville
(b) the conferring by Harvard of a Doctor of Laws upon Andrew Jackson, his successor in the White House
(c) the election by the Library of Congress of the anti-Catholic Samuel F. B. Morse as the national poet laureate
(d) the appointment of Sequoyah, who single-handedly created the Cherokee alphabet, to the position of Honorary Congressman

_____ **44**

45 ▪ Samuel Sewall, one of the judges who condemned to death nineteen persons in the witchcraft cases in Salem, Massachusetts, in 1692, later said that

(a) the whole community should have been hanged.
(b) he had been a witch—he often felt the way the condemned said they had.
(c) the convictions were a mistake.
(d) the fifty women who got off scot-free had lavished sexual pleasure on the judges.

_____ **45**

46 ▪ Through President_____'s administration, it had been a world without discovery of King Tut's tomb, a woman in the Senate, skywriting, Eskimo pie, jelly beans, the television iconoscope scanner, religious services on the radio, "I'm Just Wild About Harry," the Teapot Dome scandal, _Mein Kampf_ and the lie-detector test.

(a) Herbert Hoover
(b) William Howard Taft
(c) William McKinley
(d) Woodrow Wilson

_____ **46**

47 ▪ The only congressman to vote against U.S. entry into both the First and the Second World Wars was

(a) Jeannette Rankin.
(b) Henry Cabot Lodge, Sr.
(c) Huey Long.
(d) William Edgar Borah.

_____ **47**

48 ▪ The first medical director of the American Red Cross blood program resigned in protest

(a) because blood donations by whites were being given to blacks.
(b) because the Armed Forces, yielding to public prejudice, required that blood donations be segregated by race.
(c) when he was not allowed to distribute blood donated by Nazi "supermen" who were captured quite by chance in Holland.
(d) when women, in late 1943, were allowed to donate blood.

_____ **48**

49 ▪ Scholarly arguments based on documentation seem to indicate that Christopher Columbus (1451–1506) was

(a) an Englishman.
(b) an Arab.
(c) Jewish.
(d) a transvestite.

_____ **49**

50 ▪ The Aesthetic Singer was calling on America and one stop was in Camden, New Jersey, where he met the Good Gray Poet. He asked advice of the poet, and was told to go ahead in his mission to shatter the ancient idols. The visitor was _____ and the poet was

(a) Wilde . . . Whitman.
(b) Wordsworth . . . Whittier.
(c) Shelley . . . Bryant.
(d) Heine . . . Sandburg.

_____ **50**

51 ▪ Though the office of vice-president had been considered as superfluous as a sixth finger,_____ vice-presidents have succeeded to the presidency.

(a) four
(b) five
(c) nine
(d) thirteen

_____ **51**

52 ▪ After the Civil War_____ was tried for war crimes.

(a) no one on either side
(b) only one person
(c) every Confederate general
(d) John Wilkes Booth, standing in for the ill Jefferson Davis,

_____ **52**

53 ▪ Psychoanalysts have noted that both_____and_____experienced a dry, stunted childhood. The father was absent and the mother was domineering, egocentric, carping, with little or no interest in her son and an inability to take pleasure in his company. Visits with him became infrequent, reluctant, unrewarding; she was estranged from happiness. The son grew up unable—except in rage—"to let go."

(a) George Washington . . . Lee Harvey Oswald
(b) Abraham Lincoln . . . Woodrow Wilson
(c) Richard M. Nixon . . . Thomas A. Edison
(d) Thomas Jefferson . . . Clark Gable

_____ 53

54 ▪ Scottish-born John Paul Jones moved to the colonies

(a) to dodge a murder charge.
(b) because, in so many words, "that's where the action is."
(c) as a sailor in search of a fleet.
(d) because George Washington had promised to make him admiral in chief.

_____ 54

55 ▪ France's gift to the United States of the Statue of Liberty was financed in part by a lottery. Money for the pedestal was raised in the United States by

    (a) selling the Mona Lisa, hanging in the National Gallery, back to the Louvre.

    (b) the passing of the hat at all baseball games, professional and amateur, in 1878 and 1880.

    (c) the Vanderbilts and the Goulds; they turned over to the Liberty committee a day's receipts from their many railroad lines.

    (d) Joseph Pulitzer's vigorous exhortations in his small New York newspaper, *The World*.

_____ **55**

56 ▪ Margaret O'Neill Timberlake (1796–1879), a former bar-maid and a widow, married President Andrew Jackson's secretary of war, John Eaton, with whom it was said she had had a long affair before her first husband's death (su-icide?). The marriage was condoned by the president but was considered so scandalous by cabinet members and their wives that it caused the dissolution of the cabinet. Eaton was appointed governor of the Florida territory, and after his death in 1856, his widow Peggy

    (a) opened brothels in New York, Philadelphia and Balti-more.

    (b) sailed with Herman Melville to the South Pacific, where cannibals found both of them to their taste.

    (c) married an Italian dancing master.

    (d) moved to the Hermitage as Andrew Jackson's mistress.

_____ **56**

57 ▪ "The judicial power of the United States shall not be constructed to extend to any suit in law or equity, commenced or prosecuted against one of the United States by citizens of another State, or by citizens or subjects of any foreign state." The Eleventh Amendment was ratified in

(a) 1798.
(b) 1853.
(c) 1866.
(d) 1899.

_____ 57

58 ▪ One former president renounced the Union during the Civil War:

(a) Franklin Pierce.
(b) John Tyler.
(c) James K. Polk.
(d) Millard Fillmore.

_____ 58

59 ▪ The popular poem

> There was a little girl
> Who had a little curl
> Right in the middle of her forehead;
> And when she was good
> She was very, very good,
> But when she was bad she was horrid.

was written by

(a) Emily Dickinson.
(b) Robert Frost.
(c) Henry Wadsworth Longfellow.
(d) Carl Sandburg.

_____ **59**

60 ▪ Because most of the whites of America were also exploited by capitalism,_____declared that simply demanding the rights enjoyed by the white man would not bring blacks much further along the road to true freedom.

(a) Quentin Reynolds
(b) Ernie Pyle
(c) Roy Wilkins
(d) W. E. B. DuBois

_____ **60**

61 ▪ The term First Lady was first used to describe the wife of

(a) President John F. Kennedy.
(b) President Martin Van Buren.
(c) President George Washington.
(d) President Rutherford B. Hayes.

_____ **61**

62 ▪ On his desk in Dearborn, Michigan, the automobile magnate Henry Ford (1863–1947) kept a framed photograph of

(a) Queen Victoria.
(b) himself, a new one being taken every day.
(c) Adolf Hitler.
(d) Richard Loeb and Nathan Leopold during their trial in Chicago for the murder of Bobby Frank.

_____ **62**

63 ▪ The number one *liberty* at issue between Great Britain and the colonies that led to the economic struggle known as the American Revolution was the liberty

(a) to import women from the brothels of England, France and northwestern Germany, as prostitutes had been imported from a house of correction in France by Louisiana earlier in the century.
(b) to make money and the decision as to who should have that liberty.
(c) to send back to the mother country criminals who had been forcibly shipped to the New World.
(d) to mete out punishment for crimes committed by British troops.

_____ **63**

64 ▪ The first president to be born in the United States rather than in an English colony was

    (a) Martin Van Buren.
    (b) James K. Polk.
    (c) John Quincy Adams.
    (d) Zachary Taylor.

_____ 64

65 ▪ American history has indeed been brief. President_____ was born while George Washington was president and had a daughter who died while Harry S. Truman was president.

    (a) Ulysses S. Grant
    (b) Franklin Pierce
    (c) Andrew Johnson
    (d) John Tyler

_____ 65

66 ▪ In_____the California Supreme Court decreed that Chinese could not be accepted as witnesses in court because they were a "distinct people...a race of people whom nature has marked as inferior."

    (a) 1854
    (b) 1899
    (c) 1942
    (d) 1973

_____ 66

67 ▪ "I was not interested in and did not read about economics or politics. I was almost wholly divorced from the contemporary scene in this country. I never read a newspaper or a current magazine like *Time* or *Harpers*; I had no radio, no telephone; I learned of the stock market crash in the fall of 1929 only long after the event; the first time I ever voted was in the presidential election of 1936."

    (a) Dwight D. Eisenhower
    (b) Joe DiMaggio
    (c) Billy Rose
    (d) J. Robert Oppenheimer

_____ **67**

68 ▪ No president and only one vice-president, _____, has been sworn in outside the United States.

    (a) Alben Barclay
    (b) Thomas Jefferson
    (c) William Rufus De Vane King
    (d) Harry S. Truman

_____ **68**

69 ▪ _____ said, "I am the last president of the United States."

    (a) James Buchanan
    (b) Herbert Hoover
    (c) Lyndon B. Johnson
    (d) Woodrow Wilson

_____ **69**

70 ▪ The first time that there was popular voting for president was in

   (a) 1790.
   (b) 1812.
   (c) 1824.
   (d) 1884.

_____ 70

71 ▪ Except for President Thomas Jefferson's Louisiana Purchase, _____ added more territory to the nation than any other president.

   (a) George Washington
   (b) William McKinley
   (c) James K. Polk
   (d) Franklin Roosevelt

_____ 71

72 ▪ While in prison in Atlanta for sedition during the First World War, the railway union leader Eugene Victor Debs (1855–1926) was nominated for president by the Socialist party and received

   (a) less than a thousand votes.
   (b) nearly a million votes.
   (c) enough votes to force a runoff in the House between the Republican (Harding-Coolidge) and Democratic (Cox-Roosevelt) candidates.
   (d) all but three of the black votes cast in the nation, as far as could be determined.

_____ 72

73 ▪ If the Confederate States of America had won the Civil War,

    (a) Lincoln would have been imprisoned, Robert E. Lee made president and the capital moved to Richmond.

    (b) even more blacks would have been ambushed and captured in Africa and shipped into slavery in America.

    (c) they would have had no plans on what then to do.

    (d) slavery would have become the law in the north, too, and enacted at gunpoint if necessary.

_____ **73**

74 ▪ This naturalized American wrote the following message in 1936 for placement in a time capsule in the library wing of publisher M. Lincoln Schuster's country home: "Dear Posterity: If you have not become more just, more peaceful, and generally more rational than we are (or were)—why then, the Devil take you."

    (a) Samuel Goldwyn

    (b) Albert Einstein

    (c) Igor Stravinsky

    (d) Jim Thorpe

_____ **74**

75 ▪ The political cartoons of Thomas Nast (1840–1902) so stirred Northerners that President Abraham Lincoln referred to Nast as the Union's best recruiting sergeant in the Civil War. Nast was a champion of honesty in government, and

(a) was hanged by Tammany Hall hoodlums.
(b) represented New York in the Senate for nearly six decades.
(c) founded the *New Republic* magazine as his private drawing board.
(d) refused a half-million-dollar bribe to lay down his pen.

_____ 75

76 ▪ About nine years into the twentieth century, a Chicago doctor made a historic contribution to the history of medicine:

(a) he diagnosed a heart attack in a living patient.
(b) he found out that infected mosquitoes carried yellow fever.
(c) he proved that there was something in the monkey's bloodstream that could lead to inoculation against cancer.
(d) he demonstrated statistically that someone born in May had a longer potential lifespan than someone born in either April or June.

_____ 76

77 ▪ _____wrote, "Any memoirs of my life would rather hurt my feelings than tickle my pride whilst I lived. I had rather glide gently down the stream of life, leaving it to posterity to think and say what they please of me, than by any act of mine to have vanity or ostentation imputed to me.... I do not think vanity is a trait of my character."

    (a) Robert Sherwood
    (b) Robert Frost
    (c) Oliver Wendell Holmes, Jr.
    (d) George Washington

_____ **77**

78 ▪ "Every gun that is made, every warship launched, every rocket fired signifies in a final sense a theft from those who hunger and are not fed, those who are cold and not clothed."

    (a) Dorothy Dix
    (b) Bernard Baruch
    (c) Dwight D. Eisenhower
    (d) Norman Thomas

_____ **78**

79 ▪ The Anglo-American Aroostook "war" was declared not by the president but unprecedentedly by

    (a) the WACS.
    (b) a governor.
    (c) the vice-president.
    (d) the secretary of agriculture.

_____ **79**

80 ▪ She was the first woman to practice before the Supreme Court, representing Indian and Negro causes, and later she represented the United States at international peace conferences. Belva Ann Lockwood (1830–1917) was also unique for having

(a) run twice for the presidency.

(b) married Booker T. Washington, the first black to dine with a president (Theodore Roosevelt) in the White House.

(c) discovered, while visiting friends at the Smithsonian Observatory, the two moons of Mars.

(d) been the first woman to ride a horse alone from coast to coast *and back again*.

———— **80**

81 ▪ After his presidency, William Howard Taft (1857–1930) became

(a) the owner of a health farm in Ludlow, Vermont.

(b) chief justice of the Supreme Court.

(c) commissioner of major league baseball.

(d) president of the International Red Cross.

———— **81**

82 • _____sang, "We owe no allegiance; we bow to no throne, Our rule is law, and the law is our own."

(a) Sons of the Revolution
(b) Paul Revere's Fife and Drum Corps
(c) Green Mountain Boys
(d) The Star-spangled Banner Society

_____ **82**

83 ▪ In his native England_____was a failure several times over (cobbler, stay-maker, corset-maker, sailor), edging ever closer to the cesspool of lower-class London and debtors' prison. At the age of thirty-seven in 1774, he sailed to the colonies with both a letter of introduction from Benjamin Franklin, whose acquaintance he had made by happenstance, and an abiding hatred of the rigidly structured English society; he thought of George III as a "hardened, sullen-tempered Pharaoh" and "the Royal Brute." He coined the name the "United States of America."

(a) Charles Cornwallis
(b) Alexander Hamilton
(c) William Cobbett
(d) Thomas Paine

_____ **83**

84 ▪ While his celebrated case was in review by the Supreme Court, the slave-servant Dred Scott

(a) was hanged by a mob on Bunker Hill.
(b) was exhibited in eleven states by P. T. Barnum.
(c) became a porter in a hotel in St. Louis, was the object of much curiosity and enjoyed it.
(d) was invited to the White House by President James Buchanan for a thirty-minute "social visit."

_____ **84**

85 ▪ Christmas Bird Count was the inspiration of

    (a) Frank Chapman.
    (b) Roy Chapman Andrews.
    (c) Maxine Andrews.
    (d) Benjamin Franklin.

_____ **85**

86 ▪ The wooden United States frigate *Constitution* (1797–
)—"Old Ironsides"—was saved from the scrapyard
when

    (a) Sons and Daughters of the Revolution formed a human
        blockade around the ship and negotiated its reconstruc-
        tion.
    (b) England said that it wanted to put the ship in a maritime
        museum at Land's End.
    (c) President Andrew Jackson, in Boston to get an honorary
        degree from Harvard, personally ordered that not a plank
        of the old warhorse, tied up at the Boston Navy Yard,
        be touched.
    (d) millions of schoolchildren contributed pennies for its
        restoration.

_____ **86**

87 ▪ Eight years before he became an American citizen, Fritz Kreisler confessed

   (a) that he had helped hide Lenin in the train that carried the Red leader back to Russia in 1917.
   (b) that he had had an affair with Arthur Rubinstein.
   (c) that he had composed "little masterpieces" (as critics called them) and ascribed them to other composers.
   (d) that he had spent several months teaching Adolf Hitler how to improve his violin playing.

_____ **87**

88 ▪ British commander Charles Earl Cornwallis (1738–1805) surrendered at the last great battle of the Revolutionary War—at the little tobacco port of Yorktown, Virginia, in October 1781. A combination of the French navy and allied armies did him in

   (a) but the war continued for two more years, with no military event of importance, however.
   (b) exactly thirty minutes before General George Washington was going to raise the white flag himself.
   (c) because no reinforcements were on the way.
   (d) at the very same time that Marquis de Lafayette was retaking New York for the Revolutionaries.

_____ **88**

89 ▪ No president was

    (a) an alcoholic.
    (b) an only child.
    (c) a driven man.
    (d) close to his father.

_____ **89**

90 ▪ At the turn of the century, U.S. institutions were frying on the journalistic griddle and truth-hungry readers were devouring every word. *Munsey's, Everybody's, Cosmopolitan, Collier's, American* and the Socialist *Appeal to Reason* successfully followed the crusading lead of editor-publisher Samuel Sidney McClure's *McClure's* in challenging the public-be-damned stance of many corporations. Upton Sinclair's serialized horror story about the Chicago stockyards revealed that

    (a) red-tagged U.S. Condemned tubercular hogs were converted into table fare for the holidays.
    (b) poisoned bread and dead rats were swept together into the meat-conveyor belt and came out as sausages.
    (c) "potted chicken" was like the boardinghouse soup through which a chicken had walked with rubbers on.
    (d) men who fell into open vats went out into the world as Anderson's Pure Leaf Lard.

_____ **90**

91 ▪ The hero of the just-concluded Spanish-American War, George Dewey (1837–1917), could not fan the flame of Democratic interest in his running for president in 1900, because his wife was

(a) a black.
(b) a Catholic.
(c) a newspaper gossip columnist.
(d) a poor cook.

_____ **91**

92. ▪ Adoption of the Thirteenth Amendment, banning slavery constitutionally, was necessary because

(a) Andrew Johnson would not use the muscle of the presidency to enforce President Abraham Lincoln's Emancipation Proclamation.
(b) the Supreme Court had deemed the Emancipation Proclamation to be unconstitutional.
(c) the Emancipation Proclamation had not prevented Southern states, on readmission to the Union, from reinstituting slavery.
(d) most Northern plantation owners and farmers had not freed their slaves; some, in fact, were continuing to import shackled blacks from Africa, and even buying them from Southern owners.

_____ **92**

93 ▪ Jefferson Davis (1808–1889), the president of the Confederacy, was captured by federal troops in Georgia a month after Appomattox and held prisoner for two years in Virginia, for a time in shackles.

(a) He was pardoned by President Andrew Johnson at Christmas time 1868.
(b) He was given a choice of being hanged or living out his life behind bars, and he chose to be executed.
(c) He escaped from the courthouse and was next seen five years later on a beach in Brighton, England.
(d) He was exhibited throughout the North in a railroad cattle car open to both spectators and the weather.

_____ 93

94 ▪ The debates in the Federal Constitutional Convention in 1787 were kept secret because

(a) they might rouse the British to declare war against the colonists.
(b) the delegates did not want differences to be exaggerated by the public and therefore undermine acceptance of the final documents.
(c) the group had been dictatorially selected by George Washington and Alexander Hamilton.
(d) a rump convention might put *its* amendments to a public vote.

_____ 94

47

95 ▪ Acting midshipman Philip Spencer, the scapegrace son of a secretary of war, was hanged by the Navy

(a) to put his father on notice that he had better watch his step in granting sweetheart contracts for new warships in the last months of the First World War.

(b) by mistake; he looked exactly like the sailor who had committed mass murder on the Baltimore wharves a few hours after the Japanese attack on Pearl Harbor.

(c) for plotting a mutiny against the 126 ton brig, *Somers*.

(d) for failing to quarterback the Naval Academy's "superman" football team to an unbeaten season in 1933— the team lost to bitter-enemy West Point on a field goal in the last two seconds of the last game of the season.

_____ **95**

96 ▪ President Theodore Roosevelt (1858–1919) was awarded the Nobel Peace Prize in 1906 for

(a) putting down his "big stick" diplomacy.

(b) warning Czar Nicholas that his Baltic fleet would be ambushed by the Japanese in Tsushima Strait.

(c) mediating the Russo-Japanese War, in a treaty conclave in Portsmouth, New Hampshire.

(d) keeping U.S. marines out of the French-German war over the future of Morocco.

_____ **96**

97 ▪ The Niagara Movement at the turn of the century brought together

   (a) marathon dancers seeking a prize of $50,000—to be awarded to those who could go two weeks without stopping.
   (b) twenty-nine militant Negro intellectuals from fourteen states.
   (c) the world's "crazies," who were stopped by authorities from going over Niagara Falls in a flotilla of barrels.
   (d) northern New York State's best baseball players (with a couple of ringers from the Canadian side of the river) to prove that they should be allowed to field a nine in the National League.

_____ 97

98 ▪ At the end of a summer's wanderings,_____wrote, "Walking across this land, I have found them, little ganglions of life, promise of thousands more. The next generation will be that of the eminent village. The sun of the farmer will be no longer dazzled and destroyed by the fires of the metropolis. He will travel, but only for what he can bring back."

   (a) Walt Whitman
   (b) William Cullen Bryant
   (c) Vachel Lindsay
   (d) Henry Wadsworth Longfellow

_____ 98

99 ▪ John C. Calhoun (1782–1850), the only vice-president to serve under two presidents, resigned as Andrew Jackson's vice-president:

(a) his daughter, Sue, had secretly married a Negro.
(b) he wanted to devote full time to editorship of the Charleston (South Carolina) *Courier*.
(c) he was on the edge of being impeached for taking kick-backs from munition-makers.
(d) an erstwhile nationalist, now a States' Rightist, he would be named a South Carolina senator and lead nullification forces on the Senate floor.

_____ **99**

100 ▪ The House of Representatives in 1918 and 1920 refused to seat Wisconsin Congressman-elect Victor Berger because

(a) he was a Socialist who had vigorously opposed United States participation in the First World War.
(b) he was an alleged homosexual.
(c) he had been a deserter during the Spanish-American War.
(d) his maternal grandfather had been a conscientious objector in the Civil War.

_____ **100**

101 ▪ As president, _____ was called His Fraudulency.

(a) Richard M. Nixon
(b) Rutherford B. Hayes
(c) Andrew Johnson
(d) Herbert Hoover

_____ **101**

102 ▪ Our most distinguished First Lady, according to a poll of one hundred history professors, was

   (a) Dolley Madison.
   (b) Eleanor Galt Wilson.
   (c) Jacqueline Bouvier Kennedy.
   (d) Eleanor Roosevelt.

_____ **102**

103 ▪ He was Royal Governor of New Jersey and espoused the Loyalist cause. He was arrested and imprisoned by the Revolutionary Congress of New Jersey, and shipped to Britain in 1778 in exchange for Americans held prisoner there:

   (a) George Washington's stepson, James.
   (b) Benjamin Franklin's illegitimate son, William.
   (c) Patrick Henry's son, Peter.
   (d) Alexander Hamilton's twin brother, Paul.

_____ **103**

104 ▪ After mapping the Northwest for the Jefferson administration, Meriwether Lewis and William Clark

   (a) ran for vice-president and president, respectively, on the Pioneer ticket in 1820.
   (b) married Indian women and lived happily ever after in the Northwest Territory.
   (c) were murdered and became a governor, respectively.
   (d) published their private diaries and lived off their royalties.

_____ **104**

105 ▪ When George Washington (1732–1799) was appointed commander of the Continental Army by the Second Continental Congress on June 15, 1775,

(a) he really didn't want the position.
(b) he was the whole army.
(c) he had to win out over four ambitious contenders.
(d) he had to pay a fee of (present-day dollars) ten thousand dollars for the honor.

_____ **105**

106 ▪ The popular Manhattan cocktail—whiskey and sweet vermouth—was invented by

(a) Mary Todd Lincoln.
(b) Jacqueline Bouvier Kennedy Onassis.
(c) J. P. Morgan, Sr.
(d) Winston Churchill's mother.

_____ **106**

107 ▪ During the First World War, Robert Goldstein, the producer of the film *The Spirit of '76*, was convicted under the Espionage Act because the film

(a) portrayed Germans, though they were fighting with Washington's beleaguered army, as "good guys."
(b) didn't begin and end with the playing of "Yankee Doodle."
(c) contained scenes of atrocities committed by British soldiers during the American Revolution.
(d) presented the Loyalist viewpoint too forcefully.

_____ **107**

108 ▪ Mrs. Margaret Higgins Sanger (1883–1966), the leader of the birth-control movement, was

    (a) sterilized after an abortion.
    (b) an only child.
    (c) an orphan, and never learned who her parents were.
    (d) the tenth child in a family of eleven.

_____ **108**

109 ▪ Establishment of the Society for the Prevention of Cruelty to Children was stimulated by

    (a) Carry Nation's axe-swinging rampages through orphanages and bleak houses.
    (b) D. W. Griffith's portrayal of plantation life in his motion picture *Way Down South*.
    (c) cries of outrage at President Theodore Roosevelt's demands on his children, "Don't flinch, don't foul, hit the line hard."
    (d) Horatio Alger's account of urchin life, *Phil the Fiddler*.

_____ **109**

110 ▪ Three months after appointment in July 1775 as director-general of hospitals for General George Washington's Continental Army, Dr. Benjamin Church

    (a) begged Washington not to encamp at Valley Forge in the winter.
    (b) removed Washington's appendix and most of his teeth.
    (c) was court-martialed for spying for the British.
    (d) led a raid on whiskey stills in Maryland for "medicinal" supplies, which he then sold to the troops.

_____ **110**

111 ▪ Only once have the president and the vice-president been of different political parties:

    (a) President Abraham Lincoln and Vice-President Hannibal Hamlin.

    (b) President John Adams and Vice-President Thomas Jefferson.

    (c) President Abraham Lincoln and Vice-President Andrew Johnson.

    (d) President Andrew Jackson and Vice-President Martin Van Buren.

_____ **111**

112 ▪ John Dewey the philosopher, Charles Beard the historian, and Edward Weeks the *Atlantic* editor agreed:_____was the most influential book written by an American in the preceding half-century and was second only to *Das Kapital* as the most influential book published in the world.

    (a) *Uncle Tom's Cabin*

    (b) *Ben-Hur*

    (c) *Walden*

    (d) *Looking Backward*

_____ **112**

113 ▪ "No person shall be elected to the office of president more than twice, and no person who has held the office of president, or acted as president, for more than two years of a term to which some other person was elected president shall be elected to the office of president more than once."— The Twenty-Second Amendment was ratified in

(a) 1877.
(b) 1915.
(c) 1951.
(d) 1973.

_____ 113

114 ▪ The rocketeer Robert Goddard (1882–1945) suffered much public humiliation before man reached the moon:

(a) the Wright brothers offered to tow him around in the air.
(b) the baseball pitching ace Walter Johnson threw a rocket farther than Goddard could propel one with liquid oxygen.
(c) "Moon Rocket Misses Target by 238,799¼ Miles"— newspaper headline.
(d) "He seems only to lack the knowledge ladled out daily in high schools."—the *New York Times*, 1920.

_____ 114

115 ▪ The Boston Tea Party (1773) was principally

    (a) a strike against Britain's maintenance of the tax on tea.

    (b) an act of principle.

    (c) an example of "horseplay" that British authorities exaggerated in order to subdue the colonists at musketpoint.

    (d) a brainstorm by Benjamin Franklin to rally the recalcitrant colonists.

_____ **115**

116 ▪ After the enormous success and influence of *Uncle Tom's Cabin*, Harriet Beecher Stowe (1811–1896) wrote

    (a) a novel about economics.

    (b) about ten nights in a barroom.

    (c) a racy biography of President Abraham Lincoln.

    (d) a thinly disguised nonfiction novel about her brief (three and a half weeks) marriage to Frederick Douglass.

_____ **116**

117 ▪ After the American Revolution, the British colony of _____ was invited by the United States to become a member of the Confederation and to adopt the Articles of Confederation as its governing instrument.

    (a) Alaska

    (b) Puerto Rico

    (c) Canada

    (d) Manhattan

_____ **117**

118 ▪ At one time there were_____time standards in the nation.

(a) more than one hundred
(b) only two
(c) an undetermined large number of
(d) fifty

_____ **118**

119 ▪ In the 1850s there was a movement afoot to purchase Cuba and

(a) make it a penal colony.
(b) make it a slave state.
(c) ship all blacks in the United States, free and still enslaved, there.
(d) turn it into a baby farm, the children having by contract to grow up on the American frontier, where hands were needed.

_____ **119**

120 ▪ President Herbert Hoover's vice-president was the son of a full-blooded

(a) Indian.
(b) African.
(c) Japanese.
(d) Arab.

_____ **120**

121 • The Moore House, built around 1725 in Virginia, was the site of

   (a) negotiations leading to the end of the Revolutionary War.

   (b) the final meeting of the Booth conspirators, who three days later murdered President Abraham Lincoln.

   (c) Nazi cloak-and-dagger operations, where espionage agents put ashore by U-boats in 1942 were able to hide out there for nearly two years.

   (d) the Wright brothers' decision to put a heavier-than-air machine into the sky before authorization was issued by the Smithsonian Institution.

_____ 121

122 ▪ The commanding officer in one of the United States Army's major disasters in the field ranked_____in his West Point graduating class, 1861.

(a) third
(b) first
(c) next to last
(d) last

_____ **122**

123 ▪ "I no longer suffer from the delusion, if I ever did, which I doubt, that I have anything to add to the sum total of man's knowledge of the universe. As for giving pleasure, I can give more with a case of good Scotch and be thanked for it."

(a) Buckminster Fuller
(b) Archibald MacLeish
(c) Ernest Hemingway
(d) Albert Einstein

_____ **123**

124 ▪ In 1811_____served—all at the same time!—as the mayor of New York City, the lieutenant governor of New York State and a state senator:

(a) Peter Cooper
(b) Peter Stuyvesant
(c) Washington Irving
(d) DeWitt Clinton

_____ **124**

125 ▪ The name of the poem was "Absolute Benison" and four of the twelve lines were

Those who delighted feast on difference,
Measuring the larkspur head-higher than the rose.
Can find no benison in burials,
The only absolute that summer knows.

After it was published, the poet decided never to publish verse again.

(a) The poem became the basis for a long-running sit-com television series.

(b) The poem was accepted under the poet's real name after having been rejected when it was submitted under a pseudonym.

(c) The poet had translated the poem from the Chinese and figured that no one would find out, but someone did and the "author" was disgraced.

(d) The remaining eight lines could be read as being pornographic, and the author, prominent in society, was ostracized by book and magazine editors.

_____ **125**

126 ▪ The first president to accept in person the nomination of his party's convention rather than follow tradition and acknowledge it weeks later was

(a) Thomas Jefferson.

(b) Zachary Taylor.

(c) Grover Cleveland (the third time).

(d) Franklin D. Roosevelt.

_____ **126**

127 ▪ Donald Duncan's toy that became an instant success in 1929 was once

    (a) a weapon in the Far East.
    (b) an Australian aborigine's boomerang.
    (c) indigenous to the Laplanders.
    (d) the mouth bit used by sailors when they were being bullwhipped or having a limb amputated.

    _____ **127**

128 ▪ "Henry Adams, you have viewed the presidency from many angles, as historian, editor, educator and world-hobnobber, and two of your ancestors were presidents. What, sir, is it like to be in charge?"

    (a) "It is such a glamorous experience that I would like to be president myself."
    (b) "A life of luxury and ease. No worries."
    (c) "Power is poison."
    (d) "I must confess, after all these years I still do not know. Sorry."

    _____ **128**

129 ▪ When Franklin D. Roosevelt named Alabama Senator Hugo LaFayette Black (1886–1971) to the Supreme Court, he did not know that Black had been

    (a) the behind-the-scene genius in manipulating the Teapot Dome windfall.
    (b) charged with bigamy, and with breaking other domestic laws.
    (c) a deserter in the First World War.
    (d) a member of the Ku Klux Klan for two years.

    _____ **129**

130 ▪ Stephen A. Douglas won the Lincoln-Douglas debates of 1858 and reelection to the Senate, but lost to Abraham Lincoln in the presidential election of 1860. Douglas then

(a) became the first commissioner of professional scalping.
(b) directed the conspiracy that killed the president in 1865.
(c) never spoke to Lincoln again—they each had been a suitor of Mary Todd—and spent more than a decade protesting Lincoln's "dirty tricks."
(d) represented Lincoln in rallying the Northwest during the first months of the Civil War.

_____ **130**

131 ▪ Before he took on—and lost—presidential campaigns against Franklin D. Roosevelt (in 1944) and Harry S. Truman (1948), Thomas E. Dewey had made his reputation as a

(a) public-relations wizard.
(b) gunslinger.
(c) chef, especially of wedding cakes, in Cleveland.
(d) racket-buster.

_____ **131**

132 ▪ Not until_____was there a federal income tax.

(a) 1861
(b) 1792
(c) 1899
(d) 1943

_____ **132**

133 ▪ The Southern planter Hinton Rowan Helper (1829–1909) wrote in 1857 *The Impending Crisis*, which demonstrated the economic effects of slavery and the stupidity of slaveholders, and declared that hay, not cotton, was king.

(a) Three men in Arkansas were hanged for having copies of the book.
(b) It was the source for Harriet Beecher Stowe's incendiary *Uncle Tom's Cabin*.
(c) The author was kidnapped, tarred and feathered, and shipped in a box to England.
(d) It stimulated Nat Turner's bloody, feverish slave revolt in Southampton County, Virginia.

_____ **133**

134 ▪ Benjamin Franklin's last public act, in 1790, was

(a) turning down the electoral college's request that he be co-president with George Washington.
(b) signing a petition to Congress calling for the abolition of slavery.
(c) signing the Declaration of Independence.
(d) marrying the common-law illiterate woman who had borne him twenty-three children.

_____ **134**

135 ▪ "On Judgment Day we'll be judged by what we didn't do rather than by what we did."

(a) Lou Gehrig
(b) Frank Sinatra
(c) Louis Brandeis
(d) Fiorello La Guardia

_____ **135**

136 ▪ A_____(and American expatriate) submitted twelve thousand sources in one year alone to the first edition of the *Oxford English Dictionary.*

(a) child prodigy (four years old)
(b) chicken farmer
(c) murderer
(d) lighthouse keeper

_____ **136**

137 ▪ Barbara Fritchie probably never said "Shoot if you must this old gray head, but spare your country's flag." She was

(a) General Stonewall Jackson's daughter-in-law and a Confederate through and through.
(b) seven years old (at most) when she supposedly protested the dragging of the Union flag in the dust.
(c) ninety-five years old and bedridden.
(d) a childhood friend of P. T. Barnum, grinding out Union propaganda to rally soldiers 'round Old Glory.

_____ **137**

138 ▪ In making his very first automobile, Henry Ford (1863– 1947) overlooked one important detail:

(a) it didn't have brakes.
(b) there was no gasoline station at the other end of the village.
(c) he didn't have a fifth tire in case one ripped.
(d) the vehicle was larger than the door of the brick workshed in which it had been secretly assembled.

_____ **138**

139 ▪ Edward Everett (1794–1865), a former congressman, president of Harvard (he had tried to enroll a black student) and secretary of state, was well known for his oratorical skills, and on that November day in 1863, he delivered his best-known wartime oration. His two-hour peroration dedicating the national cemetery was followed by

(a) the assassination of President Abraham Lincoln.
(b) a two-minute address that will be long remembered.
(c) a day-long hurricane that dampened Everett's appeal.
(d) an unexpected Confederate cannonade that killed approximately one thousand spectators.

_____ **139**

140 ▪ The "Father of Texas," Stephen Austin (1793–1836), believed that Texas did not have the resources either to win or to maintain its independence, so he argued that

(a) the middle-class Anglo-Americans there move back to the East.
(b) Mexico be brought into the union, with Texas merely a county or two in the state of Mexico.
(c) Texas remain a Mexican state.
(d) Texas join California, making one large self-supporting country.

_____ **140**

141 ▪ Only one woman has been the wife of one president and the mother of another president:

    (a) Felicity Williams Johnson.
    (b) Marjorie Judson Harrison.
    (c) Abigail Smith Adams.
    (d) Sara Delano Roosevelt.

_____ **141**

142 ▪ _____ turned down bids to be George Washington's secretary of state or chief justice of the United States. But he agreed to Washington's request that he be a candidate for the House of Delegates of Virginia, and he was elected.

    (a) Patrick Henry
    (b) Thomas Randolph
    (c) Thomas Jefferson
    (d) Samuel Adams

_____ **142**

143 ▪ Technicalities kept the territory of _____ from joining the Union in 1857 and again in 1888.

    (a) Yukon
    (b) Idaho
    (c) New Mexico
    (d) Minnesota

_____ **143**

144 ▪ At the age of seventeen, William Cullen Bryant (1794 – 1878) was writing

(a) on adjoining tables *Tom Swift and His Rocketship* and *Andy Hardy Goes to the Fair.*
(b) the classic poem "Thanatopsis."
(c) the Monroe Doctrine.
(d) the first three-act drama to be produced in America— *Our American Cousin.*

_____ **144**

145 ▪ Ethan Allen defeated the British at Fort Ticonderoga, but Allen informed the Congress that he and his Green Mountain Boys had been fighting solely for

(a) control of Lake Champlain, where they had their own navy and merchant fleet.
(b) the chance to make Allen the first president.
(c) the right to incorporate New York State into Vermont.
(d) the independence of Vermont.

_____ **145**

146 ▪ Luther Burbank—Mr. Green Thumb—developed more than _____ new plant varieties.

(a) eight hundred
(b) twenty-five
(c) one hundred
(d) one thousand

_____ **146**

147 ▪ The states did not ratify two of the twelve amendments to the Constitution in the original Bill of Rights:

(a) there would never be more than fifteen states, and the president could not succeed himself.

(b) organized sports could not be played on the Sabbath, and every physically fit male must serve two years in the army.

(c) the size of the House of Representatives would be fixed, and congressmen and senators could not raise their own salaries.

(d) married women would have the franchise, and doctors could not levy a fee for their services.

_____ **147**

148 ▪ Samuel Langhorne Clemens was born under Halley's comet, in Florida, Missouri, and predicted that he would

(a) some day see astrologers burned at the stake.

(b) become king of the universe.

(c) never die.

(d) die when the comet returned seventy years later.

_____ **148**

149 ▪ During the Civil War, the Union army employed spies, one of whom, a man named Totten,

(a) was deaf, dumb and blind.
(b) was the bastard son of Jefferson Davis, president of the Confederacy.
(c) would sue the United States for back pay.
(d) was actually a turncoat, feeding information about President Abraham Lincoln's family to Confederate General Robert E. Lee personally.

_____ 149

150 ▪ Not until_____was a woman elected to a full term in the United States Senate, and she was reelected six years later.

(a) 1856
(b) 1908
(c) 1920
(d) 1932

_____ 150

151 ▪ The year was 1820. Robert Gibbon Johnson stood on the courthouse steps in Salem County, New Jersey, and announced in stentorian tones that he would there and then eat one of those "lethal" things—the "love apple"—

(a) a piece of vanilla fudge.
(b) a bumblebee.
(c) a sweet potato.
(d) a tomato.

_____ 151

152 ▪ The Chicago architect William LeBaron Jenney (1832–1907) was inspired to design tall buildings

(a) when he studied the pyramids in Egypt and Central America.
(b) when he observed how lightweight birdcage construction worked as a frame.
(c) by the promise of a $1 million contract by a real-estate tycoon in space-shy lower Manhattan.
(d) under the fanatical prodding of Frank Lloyd Wright, who then stole the concepts.

_____ **152**

153 ▪ Thomas Edison (1847–1931) tested the phonograph that he was inventing by shouting into the machine the verses of

(a) "Poor Little Buttercup."
(b) "Silent Night, Holy Night."
(c) "Mary Had a Little Lamb."
(d) "The Star-spangled Banner."

_____ **153**

154 ▪ Before writing her best-known books, *Little Women* (1868) and *Little Men* (1871), Louisa May Alcott (1832–1888)

(a) created the game of basketball.
(b) was a recluse; her only friend in the world was Emily Dickinson.
(c) wrote swashbuckling novels and served as a nurse in the Union Hospital in Georgetown.
(d) was a manic depressive, and was one of the first patients for Freud's "talking cure."

_____ **154**

155 ▪ The phrase *Founding Fathers* was coined by

(a) Warren G. Harding.
(b) Noah Webster.
(c) Harold Ross.
(d) Henry L. Mencken.

_____ **155**

156 ▪ After his decisive victory in the Revolutionary War at Yorktown in 1781, General George Washington addressed a letter to the president of the United States. The president was

(a) George Washington himself.
(b) John Adams.
(c) John Hancock.
(d) John Hanson.

_____ **156**

157 ▪ _____ wanted to make it one big nation, the United State of America, doing away with individual states altogether.

(a) Alexander Hamilton
(b) Marquis de Lafayette
(c) DeWitt Clinton
(d) Boss Tweed

_____ **157**

71

158 ▪ The famous and extraordinarily popular *A Message to Garcia*, purportedly sent by President William McKinley to a Cuban insurgent leader on the eve of the Spanish-American War,

    (a) urged the rebels to give up before war erupted.
    (b) urged that the Havana rebels bring Cuba into the Union.
    (c) was really a preachment to careless workers to shape up and show initiative.
    (d) offered a bounty on Winston Churchill's head, if he was still in Cuba when war broke out.

_____ **158**

159 ▪ When Robert E. Lee (1807–1870) took charge of the Confederacy's Army of North Virginia during the Civil War,

    (a) he had never before commanded in a major battle.
    (b) he was a "turncoat," having commanded a battalion in the Union army for the first four months of the war.
    (c) he had been the commanding general of Union forces in both the Black Hawk and Mexican Wars.
    (d) he had spent the previous seventeen years cleaning out the widely scattered pockets of Indian resistance from border to border.

_____ **159**

160 ▪ "The Ice King" was

    (a) David M. Waite.
    (b) Frederic Tudor.
    (c) Horace Pippin.
    (d) Ebenezer MacIntosh.

_____ **160**

161 ▪ Preening in his jail cell in the District of Columbia, presidential assassin_____was convinced that God had "inspired" him to slay the chief executive.

    (a) Leon F. Czolgosz
    (b) Richard Lawrence
    (c) Charles J. Guiteau
    (d) John Wilkes Booth

_____ **161**

THE ASSASSIN'S CELL—THE MORNING TOILET

Leslie's Illustrated, DECEMBER 18, 1881

73

162 ▪ "The Star-spangled Banner" was composed by

    (a) a merchantman first class.
    (b) the U. S. poet laureate.
    (c) a lawyer.
    (d) the second secretary to President James Madison.

_____ **162**

163 ▪ Early in the nineteenth century, Concord, Massachusetts, was

    (a) once again on the prowl for witches.
    (b) a hotbed of birth-control and abortion activists.
    (c) on the verge of seceding from the state and the nation.
    (d) one of the most journal-, diary- and notebook-keeping towns in America.

_____ **163**

164 ▪ What some people won't do in the search of El Dorado:

    (a) Balboa burned his ships behind him so that his men would have to stay in the New World and look for the city of gold.
    (b) the king of Saxony shipped his subjects, every last one of them, to the New World and forced them to start walking west.
    (c) Francisco Coronado trekked thousands of miles around the American West.
    (d) Cortez cut out the tongue and cut off the hands of his illiterate grandmother so that she would not reveal what they had seen and been told.

_____ **164**

165 ▪ The "Prince of Humbugs," P. T. (Phineas Taylor) Barnum (1810–1891) exhibited George Washington's "161-year-old black nurse," the Fejee Mermaid, the midget General Tom Thumb, the elephant Jumbo, promoted the concert tour of the "Swedish Nightingale," Jenny Lind and could have said, "There's a sucker born every minute." The impresario of curiosities, freaks and theatrical headliners

   (a) shot twice at President Ulysses S. Grant to get attention for his four-ring circus, the second Greatest Show on Earth, the presidency (in his mind) "being the first".
   (b) confessed on his deathbed that Washington's nurse was only 142 and that when she died on tour, his wife, Charity, disguised herself as the nurse.
   (c) helped to amputate Sarah Bernhardt's left leg, and save her life, when she was pinned to a railroad tie in the wreckage of their circus train—on the condition that she would first agree to tour under his aegis.
   (d) served in the Connecticut legislature and as mayor of Bridgeport.

_____ **165**

166 ▪ _____ once rose from a nap and asked, "Is the country still here?"

   (a) Calvin Coolidge
   (b) Curtis LeMay
   (c) Henry James
   (d) Gertrude Stein

_____ **166**

75

167 ▪ When Thomas Edison's much heralded electric-storage battery developed snafus, the Wizard of Menlo Park

(a) took the counsel of friends and continued to sell it by the carful.
(b) announced that the electric car was a bad idea anyway: the internal combustion engine was the way to go.
(c) recalled every single one and made prompt refunds.
(d) designed an automobile that ran on soybeans.

_____ **167**

168 ▪ In framing the Declaration of Independence, which freed the colonies from England, Thomas Jefferson (1743–1826) used as a model

(a) the Magna Charta.
(b) the Declaration of Talavera.
(c) the Bill of Rights passed by the English Parliament in 1689.
(d) the *Mayflower* Compact.

_____ **168**

169 ▪ The United States' first five-star general, John J. Pershing (1860–1948), was nicknamed Black Jack because

(a) he was a card shark.
(b) he had served with a "colored" regiment, the Tenth United States Calvary.
(c) his complexion had turned jet black after a tour of duty in the Gobi Desert.
(d) he had a fetish of sleeping with a mudpack on his face.

_____ **169**

ANSWERS ON PAGE 208 ■

170 ▪ If he had not been involved in the promotion of the telegraph or the introduction of the daguerreotype process into the United States, Samuel F. B. Morse (1791 – 1872) would be known today for

(a) his size—he weighed well over five hundred pounds and at least two months in every eight he had to be on a starvation diet.
(b) being the guiding spirit behind promulgation of the Emancipation Proclamation.
(c) his invention of the electric automobile.
(d) his portrait paintings.

_____ **170**

171 ▪ Forty percent of our presidents were born in either_____ or_____

(a) Maryland... Indiana.
(b) Virginia... Ohio.
(c) New York... Pennsylvania.
(d) Massachusetts... Virginia.

_____ **171**

172 ▪ _____'s earliest recollections were of "being dressed up and allowed to come down to dance for a group of gentlemen who applauded and laughed as I pirouetted before them. Finally, my father would pick me up and hold me high in the air. He dominated my life as long as he lived, and was the love of my life for many years after he died."

(a) Martha Graham
(b) Rachel Carson
(c) Katharine Hepburn
(d) Eleanor Roosevelt

_____ **172**

173 ▪ After meeting the American army's demobilization pay from his own pocket in 1783, Superintendent of Finance Robert Morris

(a) revealed that the money had been counterfeited.
(b) ended up in debtors' prison.
(c) was named first secretary of the treasury by President George Washington.
(d) designed the Seal of the United States, with a dollar sign writ large.

_____ **173**

174 ▪ _____was to President John Quincy Adams a "virago errant in enchanted armor," and it was to her that Adams gave the first quoted presidential interview.

(a) Charlotte Forten
(b) Sarah Hale
(c) Anne Royall
(d) Susan B. Anthony

_____ **174**

175 ▪ _____ said, "Stanny White was killed, but my fate was worse. I lived."

    (a) Evelyn Nesbit
    (b) Marilyn Miller
    (c) Big Bill Tilden
    (d) Marilyn Monroe

_____ **175**

176 ▪ Two foreign-born composers have appeared on American postage stamps:

    (a) Oscar Hammerstein and Richard Rodgers.
    (b) Ludwig van Beethoven and Johann Sebastian Bach.
    (c) Irving Berlin and Arnold Schönberg.
    (d) Victor Herbert and Igor Stravinsky.

_____ **176**

177 ▪ President Abraham Lincoln's secretary of state, William Seward, suggested to Lincoln that

    (a) a war with one or more European nations would unite the United States and there'd be no Civil War.
    (b) he should resign and let Jefferson Davis become president, thereby heading off "a terrible" Civil War.
    (c) somehow he and Jefferson Davis become co-presidents.
    (d) the Union strike without warning the principal Confederate (formerly United States) forts, ending the threat of a massive conflict in a matter of a week or so.

_____ **177**

178 ▪ California's redwoods were named for

(a) the first secretary of the interior.
(b) the pioneer woman who first described them in a letter to President Martin Van Buren.
(c) an Indian.
(d) a legendary "mountain man" who had stalked the Rockies in search of Big Foot.

_____ **178**

179 ▪ One of the signers of the Declaration of Independence was _____ by the British.

(a) a spy planted
(b) captured and exiled to France
(c) captured and hanged
(d) captured and imprisoned

_____ **179**

180 ▪ The Union garrison captured at Fort Sumter in the first clash of the Civil War was

(a) allowed to go free, return North and fight another day.
(b) stuffed immediately into Andersonville Prison and never heard from again.
(c) given a choice of defecting to the Southern cause or being executed.
(d) forced to work side by side with slaves in cotton fields until they, too, dropped dead.

_____ **180**

181 ▪ The only male speaker at the first women's rights convention in Seneca Falls, New York, in 1848 was

    (a) William Lloyd Garrison.
    (b) John Brown.
    (c) Frederick Douglass.
    (d) Anthony Burns.

_____ **181**

182 ▪ Not until_____did Congress authorize an annual pension for former presidents.

    (a) November 11, 1878,
    (b) September 24, 1903,
    (c) May 25, 1930,
    (d) August 25, 1958,

_____ **182**

183 ▪ _____were imported in 1856 by President Pierce's secretary of war, Jefferson Davis, to carry troops and materiel across the arid lands of the Southwest.

    (a) Llamas
    (b) Elephants
    (c) Camels
    (d) Hippos

_____ **183**

184 ▪ The first formally declared major candidate in the 1984 presidential race was once successfully sued by

(a) Mamie Eisenhower.
(b) Charles Schulz.
(c) Gary Trudeau.
(d) Adolf Hitler.

_____ **184**

185 ▪ Norman Prince, an affluent polo-playing Francophile from Massachusetts's north shore,

(a) set fire to the German dirigible *Hindenburg*, at Lakehurst, New Jersey, to protest the bayoneting of Belgian babies by Hun soldiers during the First World War.
(b) learned to fly and organized the Escadrille Americaine, which became the Lafayette Escadrille.
(c) urged the Treasury Department to do away with all taxes on men who kept at least four polo ponies in game readiness.
(d) was America's best known soldier on the rebels' side in the Spanish Civil War—Lillian Hellman and Ernest Hemingway wrote him love letters every single day for nearly three years.

_____ **185**

186 · _____has a population that is greater than that of any one of seven states and it pays more in taxes than any one of eleven states, yet its one representative in Congress cannot vote.

   (a) Luzon
   (b) Guam
   (c) The District of Columbia
   (d) Puerto Rico

_____ **186**

187 · Geronimo (1829?–1909), the Apache chieftain who had terrorized the Southwest,

   (a) became subdirector of the U. S. Bureau of Indian and Minority Affairs under President William Howard Taft.
   (b) led the parachute division of the Third Balloon Division in the Spanish-American War.
   (c) was imprisoned, then became a farmer.
   (d) was racked on the parade grounds of West Point, with the widow of General George Custer directing the torture.

_____ **187**

188 · Robert Fulton (1765–1815)—some history books to the contrary—did not invent the steamboat. He _did_ invent

   (a) the bicycle.
   (b) the ball-point quill.
   (c) a "diving boat."
   (d) the elevator.

_____ **188**

189 ▪ _____ said, "If saloons in Kansas are illegal, why can't I bust 'em!"

    (a) Jesse James
    (b) Karl Menninger
    (c) Oveta Culp Hobby
    (d) Carry Nation

_____ **189**

190 ▪ The first General of the Armies of the United States was

    (a) Andrew Jackson.
    (b) Ulysses S. Grant.
    (c) Theodore Roosevelt.
    (d) John J. Pershing.

_____ **190**

191 ▪ Not until_____ did a woman sit in a president's cabinet.

    (a) 1825
    (b) 1865
    (c) 1902
    (d) 1933

_____ **191**

192 ▪ The American industrialist_____ was awarded the Lenin Peace Prize.

    (a) Andrew Carnegie
    (b) Cyrus Eaton
    (c) S. S. Kresge
    (d) Henry Frick

_____ **192**

193 ▪ Alexis de Tocqueville and Gustave de Beaumont made their nine-month, nine-thousand-mile horseback-stage-coach-steamer odyssey through the United States and Quebec in the early 1830s principally to

    (a) set up trading representatives of French companies.
    (b) examine new prison procedures.
    (c) enlist single women for alliances with Frenchmen scheduled to arrive presently in the New World.
    (d) learn what pastimes could be adapted to Paris.

_____ **193**

194 ▪ Clyde W. Tombaugh (1906–   ) was able to see a speck moving 3.577 billion miles away and called it

    (a) The Force.
    (b) Planet X.
    (c) Clyde.
    (d) Pluto.

_____ **194**

195 ▪ _____thought that the Great Depression might be a good thing: "People will work harder, live a more moral life. Values will be adjusted and enterprising people will pick up the wrecks from less competent people."

(a) President Herbert Hoover's secretary of the treasury
(b) William Randolph Hearst
(c) Henry Luce
(d) Charlie Chaplain

_____ **195**

196 ▪ "Done" was

(a) Joe Louis' cry after smashing the German Max Schmeling to a pulp in a heavyweight boxing rematch in Yankee Stadium in 1938.
(b) Wolcott Gibbs's one-word review for _The New Yorker_ of a Broadway play that he had walked out of after only five minutes.
(c) Betty Crocker's suggestion that all cooks learn when that exact moment comes.
(d) the telegrapher's message that the golden spike had been hammered—the coasts of America at last were linked by rail.

_____ **196**

197 ▪ More than 1,000,000 votes were cast in New York in the 1884 presidential election. Grover Cleveland edged James G. Blaine for the state's thirty-six electoral votes by____ votes.

(a) 1,143
(b) nearly 1,000,000
(c) exactly 500,000
(d) a still indeterminate number.

_____ **197**

198 ▪ Only one president, the first, George Washington, has been the unanimous choice of the electoral college, and he was twice, but another president's election was marked by only one dissenting ballot. He was

(a) Thomas Jefferson.
(b) Andrew Jackson (first term).
(c) James Monroe.
(d) James A. Garfield.

_____ **198**

199 ▪ A year before the Declaration of Independence was proclaimed, the British offered amnesty to all but two colonists. The exceptions would be

(a) George Washington and Benjamin Franklin.
(b) John Hancock and Samuel Adams.
(c) Thomas Jefferson and Alexander Hamilton.
(d) Paul Revere and Benedict Arnold.

_____ **199**

200 ▪ The "I. F. Stone" of his day (1777–1839) was

    (a) Alexander Hamilton.
    (b) Benjamin Franklin.
    (c) John Hancock.
    (d) Hezekiah Niles.

_____ **200**

201 ▪ President Theodore Roosevelt's tireless, fearless chief forester, Gifford Pinchot (1865–1946), believed that

    (a) the government had no say in what became of the unsettled countryside.
    (b) the Indians must be marched off their oil-rich reservations.
    (c) the rights of the public to the natural resources outweighed private rights and must be given first consideration.
    (d) the mineral-rich Eastern and Pacific slopes of North America should not be reckoned in future planning.

_____ **201**

202 ▪ The first black fighting unit raised in the North in the Civil War was commanded by

    (a) William Lloyd Garrison.
    (b) Ralph Waldo Emerson.
    (c) Amos Alcott.
    (d) Robert Gould Shaw.

_____ **202**

203 ▪ There are_____presidential libraries and museums open to the public.

   (a) seven
   (b) twenty-six
   (c) twenty-nine
   (d) thirty-six

   _____ **203**

204 ▪ _____turned down the opportunity to become the president of another country.

   (a) Harry S. Truman
   (b) Bernard Baruch
   (c) Averell Harriman
   (d) Albert Einstein

   _____ **204**

205 ▪ Only one candidate has lost a presidential election campaign and won on a second bid:

   (a) Warren G. Harding.
   (b) Richard M. Nixon.
   (c) Millard Fillmore.
   (d) William B. McKinley.

   _____ **205**

206 ▪ The United States took by force in the _____ what it could not achieve by diplomacy.

    (a) the Mexican War
    (b) Aroostook "war"
    (c) Little Big Horn War
    (d) Battle of Fort Ticonderoga

_____ **206**

207 ▪ On the strength of his electrifying "cross of gold" speech, William Jennings Bryan (1860–1925)

   (a) became the United States' first ambassador to the League of Nations.
   (b) became at thirty-six the youngest man nominated for the presidency.
   (c) was invited by the Vicar of Rome to sit at his right hand.
   (d) convinced the small-town Tennessee jury that John Scopes should be severely punished for teaching evolution.

_____ **207**

208 ▪ The first American Jew to serve the United States government abroad was recalled because he was Jewish: "At the time of your appointment, as Consul at Tunis, it was not known that the religion which you profess would form any obstacle to the exercise of your consular functions. Recent information, however, on which entire reliance must be placed, proves that it would produce a very unfavorable effect. In consequence of which, the President [James Monroe] has deemed it expedient to revoke your commission." Mordecai Manuel Noah (1785–1851), a Philadelphia lawyer, a journalist and a playwright, then

   (a) founded the Anti-Defamation League of B'nai B'rith.
   (b) wrote a best seller, *Is There No Place on Earth for Us?*
   (c) tried to establish a homeland for Jews on an island in the Niagara River.
   (d) urged Jews never to serve Washington.

_____ **208**

209 ▪ "The manufacture, sale or transportation of intoxicating liquors is prohibited"—the Eighteenth Amendment—was ratified in

    (a) 1823.
    (b) 1834.
    (c) 1883.
    (d) 1919.

_____ **209**

210 ▪ James Wilson was

    (a) the first justice of the Supreme Court.
    (b) winner of the first Oscar for "best actor" in 1927.
    (c) the navy ensign who tried to warn the commander of Pearl Harbor that he saw Japanese planes on his radarscope.
    (d) the inventor of mass production for the slaughter of livestock in the Chicago packinghouses.

_____ **210**

211 ▪ Joseph Smith (1805–1844), founder of the Church of Jesus Christ of Latter-Day Saints, also called Mormons, was

    (a) America's first celebrated opera singer.
    (b) murdered.
    (c) the co-inventor of radio.
    (d) on the receiving end of Samuel F. B. Morse's historic telegraph message, "What hath God wrought?"

_____ **211**

212 ▪ The historian-educator Henry Adams (1838–1918) wrote, "that, two thousand years after Alexander the Great and Julius Caesar, a man like_____should be called—and should actually and truly be—the highest product of the most advanced evolution, made evolution ludicrous. One must be as commonplace as_____'s own commonplaces to maintain such an absurdity. The progress of evolution from President Washington to President_____was alone evidence enough to upset Darwin."

    (a) Grant
    (b) Arthur
    (c) Cleveland
    (d) Hayes

_____ **212**

213 ▪ A three-paragraph letter in 1813 from John Adams, our second president, to Thomas Jefferson, our third president,

    (a) suggested that they campaign in 1816 as "The Dual President."
    (b) broke a ten-year silence between the two.
    (c) argued that Jefferson should marry the Negro slave, Sally Hemmings, who had borne him five children.
    (d) discussed the private toll road being built between their retirement residences in Maryland.

_____ **213**

214 ▪ The Post Office issued its first stamps in

    (a) 1847.
    (b) 1791.
    (c) 1820.
    (d) 1892.

_____ **214**

215 ▪ Not until this century was it discovered that earth was being bombarded from all sides by a new type of radiation which the physicist Robert A. Millikan (1868–1953) in 1925 dubbed

    (a) chariots of the gods.
    (b) the spaceships of Ezekiel.
    (c) the lunar effect.
    (d) cosmic rays.

_____ **215**

216 ▪ One of the rarest of American holographs is that of

    (a) Dolley Madison.
    (b) Button Gwinnett.
    (c) Clara Bow.
    (d) David Belasco.

_____ **216**

217 ▪ Luther Halsey Gulick (1865–1918), a specialist in physical education, helped his wife organize

    (a) the Pioneer Girls of America.
    (b) the Boy Scouts.
    (c) the Girl Scouts.
    (d) the Camp Fire Girls.

_____ **217**

218 ▪ Both parents of only_____presidents lived long enough to see their son in the White House.

    (a) two
    (b) four
    (c) six
    (d) nine

_____ **218**

219 ▪ Thomas Paine's historic bestselling forty-seven-page revolutionary tract, *Common Sense*, boldly advocated the colonies' separation from England and hastened the Declaration of Independence, and his series of pamphlets, *The Crisis*, heartened the patriots with whom he fought side by side in the Revolution. On his return to Europe he

    (a) was hanged, as a British citizen, for insurrection.
    (b) had his Philadelphia solicitor sue the publishers for royalties never paid and pursue other publishers for copyright infringements.
    (c) called for the overthrow of the monarchies, causing the English to outlaw him and the French to jail him.
    (d) tried to convince Benedict Arnold to return to the States and face the music as the traitor he was.

_____ **219**

220 ■ _____'s technocracy movement was hailed as the cure for the Depression. It called for placing the government in the hands of scientists and engineers, the end of the profit system, a work year of 132 days, and a working-age span from 25 to 45 years. Funds would be raised by a 2 percent national sales tax.

(a) Dr. Francis Everett Townsend
(b) Howard Hughes
(c) Luther Burbank
(d) Lionel Trilling

_____ **220**

221 ■ Six years after Columbus (1451–1506) made the first of his four voyages west across the Great Ocean Sea to reach the riches of the "east," Vasco da Gama (c.1469–1524) skippered three ships

(a) to the very same Watling Island that Columbus had landed on in 1492.
(b) off the face of the earth—they headed west from the Canary Islands and were never seen again.
(c) round the extreme southern point of Africa, kept going and reached India—the first western Europeans to do so by sea.
(d) into New York Bay and claimed the New World for the Pope.

_____ **221**

222 ▪ Eighty-seven years before Sputnik, a space satellite was proposed by

- (a) a housewife in Salem, Massachusetts.
- (b) the chaplain of the U.S. Senate.
- (c) the explorers Lewis and Clark.
- (d) Mary Todd Lincoln.

_____ **222**

223 ▪ Harold "Whitey" Dahl (1909–1956), the best-known American flyer with the Loyalists in the Spanish Civil War, was saved from a firing squad when his "wife"

- (a) agreed to stand in his place at the stake.
- (b) turned out to have been the Insurgent Royalist Franco's half sister.
- (c) sent Franco a luscious photograph of herself, together with a plea for her husband's life.
- (d) gave herself to the eleven political chiefs of the Royalists.

_____ **223**

224 ▪ It took King Camp Gillette (1855–1932)_____years to invent and introduce the safety razor.

- (a) eight
- (b) thirteen
- (c) nearly twenty
- (d) forty-three

_____ **224**

225 ▪ Two Americans are buried in the Kremlin:

    (a) Victoria Woodhull and Joseph P. Davies.
    (b) Lowell Thomas and Theda Bara.
    (c) Dred Scott and Benedict Arnold.
    (d) William Haywood and John Reed.

_____ **225**

226 ▪ The Democratic National Convention, meeting in New York in 1924 in the middle of Prohibition, decided to change the wording of a resolution on the death in 1923 of the Republican president, Warren G. Harding:

    (a) "wet earth" became "dry bones."
    (b) "We'll drink later to his memory" was added.
    (c) "bier" became "grave."
    (d) the philandering late president had been an alcoholic and the Democrats struck that fact from the testimonial.

_____ **226**

227 ▪ The freed black Denmark Vesey

    (a) turned in the insurgent Nat Turner to the Virginia militia.

    (b) was the Negro Baseball League's home-run leader, with an average of 1.7 HRs *per game* over twenty-eight years.

    (c) led a revolt against Charleston, South Carolina.

    (d) led the American Expeditionary Force's tank corps under General "Black Jack" Pershing in France in 1918, and was slain on November 10, 1918.

_____ **227**

228 ▪ Shortly before the Declaration of Independence was drawn, George Washington

    (a) tried to get the rebels to call off the revolution.

    (b) was nearly kidnapped.

    (c) met secretly in Nova Scotia with King George to try to settle the differences to the satisfaction of the contenders.

    (d) said that he would not sign the parchment unless it was unanimously agreed "up front" by the Continental Congress that he would be the nation's first president.

_____ **228**

229 ▪ *Hans Brinker; or The Silver Skates*—the children's classic about a Dutch youth—was written by

(a) Louisa May Alcott, under a pseudonym.
(b) Emily Dickinson, in her sister Elisabeth's name.
(c) Mary Mapes Dodge of New York.
(d) Eleanor Roosevelt, as a classroom exercise when she was eleven years old.

_____ **229**

230 ▪ Samuel Carter (1819–1891) made a unique mark in the military history of the nation:

(a) he was allowed back into the Marine Corps after defecting to the Soviet Union in the 1950s.
(b) he ordered the execution of one thousand GIs who went AWOL in Italy during a six-week period of 1944 without getting approval from the corps commander, Mark Clark. "Lessons have to be taught," Carter averred, "duty must be performed."
(c) he served in high ranks of both the army and the navy.
(d) he won three Congressional Medals of Honor.

_____ **230**

231 ▪ "I recognize that education, when conducted along sane and practical, as opposed to dogmatic and theoretical, lines, is, next to religion, the great civilizing influence."

(a) James Buchanan Duke
(b) John Dewey
(c) James Conant
(d) Robert Hutchins

_____ **231**

232 ▪ Prominent slaveholders like John C. Calhoun, Henry Clay and Andrew Jackson supported

(a) a plan for Congress to help establish an African colony to which two hundred thousand American blacks could be sent.
(b) John Quincy Adams's proposal to give each slave $500 and immediate freedom.
(c) Patrick Henry's plan to import another million black slaves "and call it a day."
(d) mass castration and sterilization of all blacks who chose not to return to Africa by year's end.

_____ **232**

233 ▪ _____was a sixteen-year-old runaway white slave, and there were advertisements in newspapers offering a ten-dollar reward to get him back.

(a) Noah Webster
(b) Henry Clay
(c) Andrew Johnson
(d) Robert Fulton

_____ **233**

234 ▪ Between 1920 and 1924, Helen Keller (1880–1968) ventured into

(a) writing cookbooks.
(b) painting.
(c) the operation of a school for young trapeze performers.
(d) vaudeville.

_____ **234**

235 ▪ During her lifetime, Emily Dickinson (1830–1886) allowed only_____of her poems to be published.

  (a) two
  (b) seven
  (c) twenty-six
  (d) ninety-four

_____ **235**

236 ▪ The mother of the founder of Harvard College was from

  (a) Moscow.
  (b) Jerusalem.
  (c) Keifeng, China.
  (d) Stratford-upon-Avon.

_____ **236**

237 ▪ Construction of the 555-foot Washington Monument was suspended for twenty-six years at the 153-foot level when

  (a) it turned out that a block of the marble was from Rome's Temple of Concord—a gift from Pope Pius IX.
  (b) Congress changed its mind and wanted to call it the Columbus Monument, causing a national furor.
  (c) the original design reminded the feminists Amelia Bloomer and Victoria Woodhull of a phallus, and they raised holy hell.
  (d) the War Department revealed that the shaft could be bowled over easily by a cannonball in any future war.

_____ **237**

238 ▪ The United States did not have its first woman governor until

    (a) 1834.
    (b) 1858.
    (c) 1926.
    (d) 1949.

_____ **238**

239 ▪ The heaviest drinking by Americans took place between

    (a) 1929 and 1937.
    (b) Fort Sumter and Appomattox.
    (c) the 1790s and the 1830s.
    (d) the Boston Tea Party and Yorktown.

_____ **239**

240 ▪ Colonel George Washington quit his commission in the Virginia militia

    (a) so he could pursue full time his romance with Patrick Henry's widow.
    (b) when his mother insisted on going to brigade balls as his "date."
    (c) when he didn't get a commission in the regular British army.
    (d) when his commanding officer wanted to reassign him to either Canada or India.

_____ **240**

241 ▪ It is agreed by historians that at least two bona fide psychopaths have run for the presidency:

(a) George McClellan and William Jennings Bryan.
(b) Horace Greeley and Ambrose Bierce.
(c) Father Coughlin and Huey Long.
(d) Rufus King and Raphael Peale.

_____ **241**

242 ▪ After publishing at the age of twenty-four the critically acclaimed literary sensation *The Red Badge of Courage*, in 1895, Stephen Crane

(a) wrote *The Yellow Badge of Cowardice*, which never got published.
(b) never wrote another word.
(c) wrote two more successful novels, *The Clansman* and *The Trail of the Lonesome Pine*.
(d) died at the age of twenty-eight of drunkenness, general depravity and tuberculosis.

_____ **242**

243 ▪ Until the First World War, the most widely taught foreign language in American schoolrooms was

(a) Yiddish.
(b) German.
(c) the Irish brogue.
(d) French.

_____ **243**

244 ▪ Street violence in the nineteenth century was as American as cherry pie. In 1844, American Republicans in tall beaver hats rioted in Philadelphia and burned two Catholic churches. The American Republicans were the forerunners of the

(a) Borzois.
(b) Health and Sunshine Society.
(c) Know-Nothings.
(d) Knights Templars.

_____ **244**

105

245 ▪ The park that architects Frederick Law Olmsted and Calvert Vaux began shaping in 1857 and that serves today as the model for other public areas is larger than

(a) Luxembourg.
(b) Gibraltar.
(c) the Canal Zone.
(d) Monaco.

_____ 245

246 ▪ After coaching the University of Oklahoma football team, Vernon L. Parrington (1871–1929) turned his hand to academic pursuits and

(a) composed tunes for singing the United States Constitution and the Bill of Rights.
(b) taught seven science subjects a day for the next forty-two and a half years.
(c) wrote *Main Currents in American Thought*, which was awarded the Pulitzer Prize in history in 1928.
(d) published a much-reprinted treatise on the social and moral evils of football.

_____ 246

247 ▪ _____presidents of the United States did not attend college.

(a) Three
(b) Seven
(c) Nine
(d) Seventeen

_____ 247

248 ▪ The black abolitionist Frederick Douglass (1817–1895), who had adopted the surname Douglass from a figure in a novel by Walter Scott, thought unwise his friend John Brown's raid on the United States arsenal at Harpers Ferry, Virginia, in October 1859. (Brown had hoped to inspire a general slave insurrection, but no blacks arrived to support him. He and his small band surrendered to United States Marines under Colonel Robert E. Lee, and Brown was hanged.) Douglass preferred Brown's earlier plan:

(a) establishment of a guerrilla base in the Appalachians.
(b) a lightning raid on Congress, kidnapping as many Southern legislators as possible.
(c) a plantation-by-plantation tour of the South with President James Buchanan, with the journalists in tow.
(d) a duel with Jefferson Davis, the survivor determining the future of slavery.

_____ **248**

249 ▪ A few days before the showman (and politician) P.T. Barnum died in 1891,

(a) he bequeathed his curiosities, freaks and theatrical headliners to the Republican Party.
(b) the New York _Evening Sun_ published his obituary.
(c) he revealed that he was a twin and that the original P.T. had died a score of years earlier—not even P.T.'s wife had caught on.
(d) made the first successful parachute jump from the torch of the Statue of Liberty.

_____ **249**

250 ▪ The first scientific magazine to publish an account of the Wright brothers' first flights in an airplane was

(a) *Gleanings in Bee Culture.*
(b) *Scientific American.*
(c) *Science.*
(d) *London Astronomy.*

_____ **250**

251 ▪ The first million-dollar contract in the United States was for

(a) paintings being sold by the Hermitage.
(b) slaves from Africa.
(c) armaments.
(d) construction of prisons, at least one in each of the original Thirteen Colonies.

_____ **251**

252 ▪ A popular Wobblie cartoon showed a father and a son sharing a lathe. The caption:

FATHER: Just work hard for the next twenty years, son, and maybe you'll be where I am now.
SON: Where's that, pop?
FATHER:_____

(a) Shop steward.
(b) Married to the prettiest woman in town.
(c) On this side of the machine.
(d) Sharing a lathe with you and your son.

_____ **252**

253 ▪ Sigmund Freud wrote that President_____"felt himself in direct communication with God. He felt that God had chosen him for a great work and would use and preserve him until his work was done."

    (a) Abraham Lincoln
    (b) Franklin Roosevelt
    (c) Woodrow Wilson
    (d) Grover Cleveland

_____ **253**

254 ▪ Until_____the individual states set their own date for presidential elections.

    (a) 1812
    (b) 1845
    (c) 1884
    (d) 1912

_____ **254**

255 ▪ Because it was impossible to divest "Typhoid Mary" (Mary Mallon) of the bug she was carrying which was causing infection and death through at least seven epidemics in Manhattan,

    (a) she was exhibited worldwide in a glass cage by P.T. Barnum and his successor.
    (b) she was executed in the tenderloin district of Broadway and her body quickly cremated.
    (c) she was quarantined by health authorities for the last twenty-three years of her life.
    (d) she was not allowed to keep her nineteen children in her home.

_____ **255**

256 ▪ The vice-president of the Confederacy

    (a) was not allowed by the Senate to take his seat after the Civil War.

    (b) joined with the Confederate president, Jefferson Davis, in trying to re-form the union of Southern states (1875–1876).

    (c) was implicated in the plot to assassinate President Abraham Lincoln.

    (d) fled to Mexico after Appomattox, and later helped to recapture Texas for Mexico for a three-week period in 1873.

_____ **256**

257 ▪ When James Monroe (1758–1831) and Robert R. Livingston (1746–1813) sailed separately for Paris in the early 1800s, their mission was

    (a) to sell six of the western states back to Napoleon.

    (b) to offer Napoleon command of American forces in the looming war against Britain.

    (c) to buy a small piece of French-held land in the Southwest—New Orleans–and to expand waterway traffic.

    (d) to convince the Marquis de Lafayette to be a candidate for president in 1808.

_____ **257**

258 ▪ Sheriff Henry Plummer's law-enforcement area included the gold-mining camps of Virginia City, Diamond City and Bannack in southwestern Montana, at the time (early 1860s) in Idaho Territory. He was also

(a) a woman.
(b) a black.
(c) an outlaw.
(d) a spy for the Sioux.

_____ **258**

259 ▪ Through President_____'s administration, it had been a world without the safety match, an advertising agency, Seventh-Day Adventists, *The Three Musketeers*, *Giselle*, a minstrel show troupe, use of ether as anesthetic during surgery, the Webster-Ashburton Treaty, Gogol's *Dead Souls*, Fremont's survey of the Oregon Trail and the creed that religion is the opium of the people.

(a) William Henry Harrison
(b) John Quincy Adams
(c) Benjamin Harrison
(d) James Polk

_____ **259**

■ ANSWERS ON PAGE 223

260 ▪ During Prohibition, Police Commissioner Grover Whalen counted_____speakeasies in New York City.

    (a) exactly one hundred
    (b) thirty-two thousand
    (c) "about a million"
    (d) zero

_____ **260**

261 ▪ Before Fort Sumter—a symbol of national authority—was shelled and captured by the Confederates, setting off the Civil War, the president-elect, Abraham Lincoln,

    (a) said that he would visit Charleston, South Carolina, the site of the fort, and personally mend the fray.
    (b) announced, "Let the war begin," for he was of the strongly held view that the war would inevitably erupt but that it could be short-lived.
    (c) offered to exchange Sumter for the Confederate bastion near Williamsburg, Virginia.
    (d) offered to evacuate the fort, and decided instead to reinforce it.

_____ **261**

262 ▪ "The Lake is there, awaiting, in all its glory; and the sky is there above, awaiting in its eternal beauty; and the Prairie, the ever-fertile Prairie is awaiting. And they, all three, as a trinity in one, are dreaming—some prophetic dream." So Louis Sullivan

  (a) set fire to Milwaukee.
  (b) arranged that Congress establish a naval academy in Salt Lake City.
  (c) designed buildings for Chicago that were great in influence and power and "summed up all truth in Art."
  (d) authorized, as governor of Indiana, the extension into Indian-held territories of the New York Central Railway.

_____ 262

263 ▪ "Watson, please come here, I want you" were the first words heard on the telephone, and Thomas A. Watson came rushing from another floor, where he had been hooking up an instrument, to the aid of the caller, Alexander Graham Bell, who had spilled battery acid on his pants. Bell had been working to improve the telegraph and had invented the telephone accidentally. At another historic moment, thirty-nine years later in 1915, Bell again called out, "Watson, please come here, I want you," but Watson didn't come this time:

(a) it was the first transcontinental call.
(b) the seance didn't work.
(c) Bell's assistant, his head having been stomped by retreating horses in the Spanish-American War, was too deaf to hear the command.
(d) Watson had had enough of old man Bell's demands; besides, he had not been given the promised five thousand shares of stock in Bell & Edison Telephone and Telegram, Inc. And so he barked into the phone, "We all know that Philipp Reis invented the telephone in Germany in 1860, so come off it, you charlatan."

_____ **263**

264 ▪ _____ believed that "we are responsible, not our leaders, since we follow them."

(a) Clarence Darrow
(b) Felix Frankfurter
(c) Salmon P. Chase
(d) Lincoln Steffens

_____ **264**

265 ▪ Over President_____'s veto, blacks were given the vote in Washington, D.C.

   (a) Rutherford B. Hayes
   (b) Chester A. Arthur
   (c) William Howard Taft
   (d) Andrew Johnson

_____ **265**

266 ▪ Winfield Scott was considered to be

   (a) the power behind Abraham Lincoln's successful presidential campaigns.
   (b) the greatest United States general between Yorktown and Bull Run.
   (c) the secret courier who took the message to Garcia.
   (d) the geologist who discovered fragments of the Uranus meteor on the shores of both Lake Superior and Lake Erie in 1933.

_____ **266**

267 ■ _____was our fattest president. One day, Paul F. Boller, Jr., has written, he went swimming in the Atlantic and friends decided to join him. But on second thought, one said, "Perhaps we'd better wait, the president is using the ocean." He was also a very polite man; on streetcars he would rise and give his place to three women.

    (a) Benjamin Harrison
    (b) Herbert Hoover
    (c) William Howard Taft
    (d) Grover Cleveland

_____ **267**

268 ■ The novel about tenement life on the lower East Side of New York disappeared from print soon after publication, but on republication thirty years later in 1964, it sold more than a million copies.

    (a) _Waiting for Lefty_
    (b) _The Great Gatsby_
    (c) _From Here to Eternity_
    (d) _Call It Sleep_

_____ **268**

269 ■ The villains in Harriet Beecher Stowe's mild abolitionist tract, _Uncle Tom's Cabin_, which was, nevertheless, a trigger of the Civil War, were

    (a) blacks who had escaped from the Dominican Republic.
    (b) the plantation ladies who had had affairs with slaves.
    (c) Northern renegades.
    (d) President Abraham Lincoln's brothers-in-law, who were Dixie through and through.

_____ **269**

270 ▪ The March of Dimes, the national fund-raising campaign for combating infantile paralysis, was launched with the active support of

    (a) Joe Louis.
    (b) Gertrude Ederle.
    (c) Franklin D. Roosevelt.
    (d) Charles A. Lindbergh.

_____ **270**

271 ▪ The music that became the number-one rock 'n' roll hit, "It's All in the Game," was written by

    (a) Lou Gehrig.
    (b) Wilt Chamberlain.
    (c) Vice-President Charles G. Dawes.
    (d) Mary Eddy Baker.

_____ **271**

272 ▪ In the 207-year history of the country, a majority of voting-age population has_____elected the president.

    (a) at no time
    (b) five times
    (c) eight times
    (d) thirteen times

_____ **272**

273 ▪ Although he had generaled the Union to a smashing triumph in the Civil War, Ulysses S. Grant (1822–1885) was not confirmed by Congress to be

(a) the ruling military authority stationed in the South.
(b) commander in chief of all the armed forces.
(c) commandant of West Point.
(d) secretary of war.

_____ **273**

274 ▪ When G. Stanley Hall (1844–1924), the president of Clark University in Worcester, Massachusetts, doubled the expense allowance to seven hundred fifty dollars,_____ agreed to deliver several lectures there.

(a) Sigmund Freud
(b) Lenin
(c) Mao
(d) Adolf Hitler

_____ **274**

275 ▪ When sculptor Horatio Greenough's marble statue of George
Washington—sitting, half-nude (the top half), a napkin
on his lap, sandals on his feet—was unveiled in the rotunda
of the capitol in 1841,

    (a) critics praised the work and the uneducated public was
indignant.

    (b) it fell through the wooden floor, killing thirteen school-
children and four teachers.

    (c) it was presently bombarded with buckshot by (it is
thought to this day) British tourists.

    (d) Daughters of the American Revolution knocked its
block off.

_____ 275

276 ▪ The spy Nathan Hale (1755–1776), executed without a
trial, is remembered for having said, "I only regret that I
have but one life to lose for my country," but his last
words, according to a British officer, really were

    (a) "I must say Samuel Johnson was right; impending
death certainly sets the mind."

    (b) "It is the duty of every good officer to obey any orders
given him by his commander in chief."

    (c) "Tell General Washington that I shall think about him
always."

    (d) "It's a mistake, it's all a mistake."

_____ 276

277 ▪ Thomas Edison (1847–1931) invented many products, but made only one purely scientific discovery:

(a) it made it possible for an electric light bulb to burn until the end of time—industrialists persuaded the dying Edison to destroy the blueprints.
(b) it stood on its head the laws of gravity.
(c) it involves the flow of electricity across a vacuum.
(d) it allows measurement of heat in the bowels of the sun.

_____ **277**

278 ▪ After failing to reach the North Pole at the turn of the century, Commander Robert E. Peary (1856–1920) wrote that his dream of sixteen years was ended. "I made the best fight I knew. I believe it has been a good one. But I cannot accomplish the impossible." Peary then

(a) founded the Bird's Eye frozen food company.
(b) tried to reach the South Pole, succeeding by zeppelin a year before he died.
(c) set out again for the North Pole, which he would (mistakenly) announce that he had finally reached.
(d) retired to his farm in Oklahoma and spent a dozen years watching the clouds (he saw them as glaciers) drift by.

_____ **278**

279 ▪ In the wake of the worldwide publicity of the "monkey trial," John Thomas Scopes (1900–1970)

    (a) became an adviser in prosecuting attorney William Jennings Bryan's third presidential campaign.

    (b) chose not to "capitalize on [his] publicity and reap the monetary harvest that was close at hand."

    (c) teamed up with his defense lawyer, Clarence Darrow, and Ben Hecht and wrote the play *Inherit the Wind.*

    (d) delivered a speech every night (except for the Sabbath) for just over a year.

_____ **279**

280 ▪ At his death in 1935, the former Pullman-car porter George Young

    (a) donated his collection of nine thousand books to the New York Public Library.

    (b) had his ashes spread over the Pullman factory, near Chicago.

    (c) was 165 years old.

    (d) turned out to have been a white man.

_____ **280**

281 ▪ After delivering in a snowfall the longest inaugural address—nearly two hours—our ninth president, William Henry Harrison,

   (a) couldn't talk for nearly three months.

   (b) insisted that his grandson Benjamin make the same address, if he, too, became president, and he did.

   (c) swore that he would never make another public speech while in office, with but one exception—at his second inauguration.

   (d) came down with pneumonia and died a month later.

_____ **281**

282 ▪ Before becoming an industrial magnate and one of the richest men in the United States, the Scottish-born (Dunfermline) Andrew Carnegie

   (a) had thought of the safety pin but didn't figure out how to make it.

   (b) was a hobo, and was on hand when the golden spike joining east and west railroad trackage was driven.

   (c) was superintendent of the eastern military and telegraph lines, performing notable services for Union armies during the Civil War.

   (d) flipped a coin and lost all of the oil rights east of the Mississippi to John D. Rockefeller.

_____ **282**

283 ▪ "Okay," Commodore Stephen Decatur said, "you're near-sighted, so I'll accommodate you." So he and Captain James Barron agreed to a pistol duel at only eight paces, and

(a) the naval hero of Tripoli and the War of 1812 was fatally shot.

(b) both men shot at the same moment and both were killed.

(c) Barron still couldn't see properly and accidentally shot Decatur's second.

(d) they both missed and went off arm in arm, saying, "May she always be in the right; but our country, right or wrong."

_____ **283**

284 ▪ Henry Schoolcraft, leading a government research party, discovered the source of the Mississippi River_____years after the lower Mississippi had been discovered.

(a) more than four hundred

(b) nearly three hundred

(c) less than two

(d) about thirty-five

_____ **284**

JOURNAL OF A VOYAGE, LIBRARY OF CONGRESS

■ ANSWERS ON PAGE 227

285 ▪ Congress granted_____to Meriwether Lewis (1774–1809) and William Clark (1770–1838) to explore a land route to the Pacific Ocean.

(a) $1,000,000
(b) $2,000,000
(c) $1 apiece
(d) $2500

_____ **285**

286 ▪ _____ wrote, "I have ever acted from a Principle of Love to my Country Since the commencement of the present unhappy Contest between Great Britain and the Colonies. The same Principle of Love to my Country actuates my present conduct, however it may appear inconsistent to the World, who very seldom judge right of any man's actions."

    (a) Aaron Burr
    (b) Nathaniel Bacon
    (c) Benjamin Banneker
    (d) Benedict Arnold

_____ **286**

287 ▪ The first fatalities in the Civil War were

    (a) two of Abraham Lincoln's brothers-in-law.
    (b) Massachusetts militiamen marching through Baltimore.
    (c) two secessionist Southern senators, assassinated as they were packing up to leave Washington for good.
    (d) the Union garrison at Fort Sumter, in Charleston harbor.

_____ **287**

288 ▪ The Pilgrims landed on Cape Cod in 1620, but they weren't known as Pilgrims until

    (a) the next year, when the hearty band was so named by a Pequoit child.
    (b) 1669.
    (c) 1637, so named by the founder of Harvard College.
    (d) 1934, when their original name, Honkies, took on a pejorative connotation.

_____ **288**

289 ▪ Joseph Smith (1805–1844) founded the Church of Jesus Christ of Latter-Day Saints—the Mormons—in

   (a) Fayetteville, New York.
   (b) Charleston, West Virginia.
   (c) Lincoln, Nebraska.
   (d) Salt Lake City, Utah.

_____ **289**

290 ▪ At his death in November 1832, _____ was ninety-five years old, the last surviving signatory to the Declaration of Independence and the nation's wealthiest man.

   (a) Lyman Hall
   (b) Joseph Hewes
   (c) Charles Carroll
   (d) Caesar Rodney

_____ **290**

291 ▪ "Public service is my motto" was professed by

   (a) Fiorello La Guardia.
   (b) Al Capone.
   (c) Norman Thomas.
   (d) Dorothy Parker.

_____ **291**

292 ▪ "I have not the advantage of a classical education, and no man should, in my judgment, accept a degree he cannot read." And so President_____, dreading the ridicule of unruly Oxford students, declined an honorary law degree from the chancellor of Oxford University.

    (a) Millard Fillmore
    (b) Andrew Jackson
    (c) Calvin Coolidge
    (d) Harry S. Truman

_____ **292**

293 ▪ Wilbur and Orville Wright_____to choose which of them would be the first man to try to fly in a heavier-than-air machine that December day in 1903 at Kitty Hawk, North Carolina.

    (a) did not know how
    (b) threw a stone at a tin can
    (c) had their father along
    (d) tossed a coin

_____ **293**

294 ▪ _____months after assuming his first elective office, Chester A. Arthur (1830–1886) became the twenty-first president.

    (a) Seventy-six
    (b) Seventeen
    (c) Thirty-two
    (d) Six

_____ **294**

295 ▪ Identifying the pilot as a guest of the United States and asking that he be given safe passage, the first airborne letter was written by

(a) George Washington.
(b) Henry Raymond.
(c) Samuel F. B. Morse.
(d) Madam Jamal.

_____ **295**

296 ▪ His achievements exercised an important influence on the shift of the Southern agricultural economy from a single-crop basis (cotton) to a diversified and more prosperous foundation:

(a) Jefferson Davis.
(b) Lyndon B. Johnson.
(c) George Washington Carver.
(d) Booker T. Washington.

_____ **296**

297 ▪ "Will anyone remember me?" was asked by

(a) J. D. Salinger.
(b) Judge Joseph Crater.
(c) "Wrong-way" Corrigan.
(d) the Marquis de Lafayette.

_____ **297**

298 ▪ When he told the Republican committee that he was as clean as a hound's tooth, not to worry, he could safely be nominated for the presidency, he was lying.

    (a) Abraham Lincoln.
    (b) Warren G. Harding.
    (c) Dwight D. Eisenhower.
    (d) Richard M. Nixon.

_____ **298**

299 ▪ The free-spirited dancer Isadora Duncan (1878–1927) asked _____ to father a child with her.

    (a) Edwin Arlington Robinson
    (b) Douglas Fairbanks
    (c) Harpo Marx
    (d) Woodrow Wilson

_____ **299**

300 ▪ President James A. Garfield had planned to make General Lew Wallace (1827–1905) the American minister to Paraguay. But then he read Wallace's *Ben-Hur* and decided to send him instead to _____ where he might be stimulated to compose another bestseller about biblical times.

    (a) Cairo
    (b) Rome
    (c) Jerusalem
    (d) Constantinople

_____ **300**

301 ▪ On Easter Sunday 1939, the Daughters of the American Revolution would not allow Marian Anderson, the black opera singer, to give a concert in Constitution Hall in the nation's capital. As a result,

(a) Miss Anderson refused to give a concert anywhere ever again in the United States—five years later, however, she changed her mind.
(b) membership in the D.A.R. soared.
(c) the First Lady, Eleanor Roosevelt, resigned from the D.A.R. and arranged for Miss Anderson to present her concert from the steps of the Lincoln Memorial.
(d) Miss Anderson never again visited Washington.

_____ **301**

302 ▪ When Dr. Jesse William Lazear allowed himself to be bitten by an infected mosquito,

(a) his death helped to convince the Yellow Fever Commission that it was on the right track.
(b) he didn't get sick for even an hour, thus disproving the key theory of the Yellow Fever Commission.
(c) he unexpectedly came down with polio.
(d) the American Medical Association said that medical men must not become guinea pigs, and took away Dr. Lazear's license to practice.

_____ **302**

303 ▪ An incensed Wendell Phillips (1811–1884) converted to abolitionism and became the cause's principal activist after

    (a) his daughter was not allowed to marry a black minister.

    (b) being forced to hang a Negro family of seven as a "lesson" to the community of Chazy, New York.

    (c) seeing the abolitionist William Lloyd Garrison dragged down a street in Boston with a rope around his neck.

    (d) reading *Uncle Tom's Cabin* for the fifth time.

                             _____ **303**

304 ▪ The indefatigable Vice-President Hannibal Hamlin (1809–1891) of Maine encouraged the Emancipation Proclamation, the removal of General George McClellan for his inept command of the Union Army and the formation of emancipated slaves into Union battalions—his son served with one of the black battalions. In 1864 he

    (a) campaigned for Christmas as a national holiday.

    (b) fled to Montgomery, Alabama, and helped Jefferson Davis rally black slaves to the Confederate cause.

    (c) was dumped as Abraham Lincoln's vice-presidential running mate.

    (d) demanded that Congress impeach the slow-acting president.

                             _____ **304**

305 ▪ The Constitution provides for the establishment of embassies abroad, but it wasn't until_____that the first ambassadors were appointed.

(a) 1933
(b) 1919
(c) 1893
(d) 1829

_____ **305**

306 ▪ "Coxey's army"—numbering at one time twenty-thousand unemployed men—walked from Massillon, Ohio, to the nation's capital in the spring of 1894 to demand jobs:

(a) everyone was arrested for living off the land and only three men, disguised as women, made it to Washington, where they were promptly arrested as transvestites.
(b) all six hundred of the men who made the complete hike were given civil service jobs back in Massillon and other home towns.
(c) before Mayor Jacob Coxey could make his speech demanding public building programs, he was arrested by police for walking on the grass.
(d) the supplicants were tarred and feathered by the army and District police who were called out by President Grover Cleveland, and run out of town.

_____ **306**

307 ▪ President_____urged Congress to use its "best endeavors to improve the education and manners of a people to accelerate the progress of art and science; to patronize works of Genius, to confer rewards for inventions of utility and to cherish institutions favorable to humanity."

  (a) John Tyler
  (b) George Washington
  (c) Calvin Coolidge
  (d) William B. McKinley

_____ **307**

308 ▪ President Grover Cleveland (1837–1908), who served two nonconsecutive four-year terms (1885–1889, 1893–1897) was once

  (a) the owner of a brothel.
  (b) suspended from the bar for bribing the judiciary of Buffalo.
  (c) a hangman.
  (d) a professional baseball player.

_____ **308**

309 ▪ _____presidents did not win their party's renomination.

  (a) Three
  (b) Five
  (c) Seven
  (d) Thirteen

_____ **309**

310 ▪ _____lived for three years in one room over a bar in Philadelphia.

(a) Thomas A. Edison
(b) "Public Enemy Number One" Clyde Barrow
(c) A future U. S. president
(d) A future king of France

_____ 310

311 ▪ The physicist who discovered that heat was a form of motion and was the first to set a figure for what is now called the mechanical equivalent of heat, and who invented a double boiler, a drip coffeepot and a kitchen range

(a) was killed by lightning at the age of fifteen.
(b) lived one hundred and one years and was the father of gerontology.
(c) spied on his fellow Americans for the British in the Revolutionary War.
(d) developed a spaceship that reached the ionosphere—in 1807.

_____ 311

312 ▪ It took the Democratic National Convention_____ballots to nominate John William Davis as its presidential candidate in 1924.

(a) 51
(b) 76
(c) 103
(d) 0 (the nomination being unanimous by voice vote)

_____ 312

313 ▪ *Spiritual Milk for Boston Babes in Either England Drawn from the Breasts of Both Testaments for Their Souls' Nourishment* was

(a) the phrase that all contestants in the first, second and fourth Miss America contests had to be able to say flawlessly in three languages.

(b) a brochure distributed by Margaret Mead and Margaret Sanger when they were colleagues in the late 1920s.

(c) the title of the first children's book printed in America.

(d) Paul Revere's creed stitched on quilts popular in maidens' bedrooms in colonial New England.

_____ **313**

314 ▪ William Walker's plan was to conquer Central America, and the pro-slavery adventurer got as far as becoming

(a) the owner of one thousand plantations in Honduras.

(b) the U.S. ambassador to each and every one of the countries there.

(c) the owner of upward of half a million slaves, black and white, who had escaped from American owners, and shaping them into an army.

(d) the "colonizer" and president of Nicaragua.

_____ **314**

315 ▪ Counties of western Virginia became the state of West Virginia in 1863 when

(a) they resolutely refused to join the rest of Virginia in seceding from the Union.

(b) Union troops, by prearrangement, raised the Stars and Stripes over every city, town and hamlet on the same day.

(c) President Abraham Lincoln, needing more ablebodied men in the army, issued an executive order that the state be formed and its eligible men mustered.

(d) the citizens' votes for secession were counted as votes against secession and for statehood.

_____ **315**

316 ▪ George "Little Mac" McClellan, removed by President Abraham Lincoln for being overly cautious as General of the Army of the Potomac, almost defeated Lincoln in the presidential election of 1864:

(a) two weeks before the election, word circulated that McClellan still had slaves on his farm in northwestern Pennsylvania.

(b) many Democratic voters did not forgive him for repudiating the party's "stop the war" appeal.

(c) Union field victories preceded the election, rejuvenating the Republican campaign.

(d) caricatures in daily and weekly newspapers were so devastating that McClellan lost through the power of the pen.

_____ **316**

317 ∙ In 1925, when she boarded a steamer in San Francisco for Honolulu and then for the Samoan Islands south of the equator where she would study the role of the adolescent girl in the primitive Polynesian society, Margaret Mead, only twenty-four years old,

(a) hoped to find the missing Amelia Earhart.
(b) had really wanted to stay home, get married and settle down on the family homestead in Pennsylvania.
(c) had been shanghaied but made the most of it.
(d) had never before traveled outside the United States, much less stayed at a hotel overnight.

_____ 317

318 ∙ _____ believed that "one of the most formidable obstacles to the cause of peace in this country is the glory of the Revolutionary War."

(a) William Ladd
(b) Elijah P. Lovejoy
(c) Theodore Roosevelt
(d) Norman Thomas

_____ 318

319 ∙ _____ warned that "the quickest way to kill broadcasting is to include advertising."

(a) Father Coughlin
(b) Grantland Rice
(c) H. V. Kaltenborn
(d) Herbert Hoover

_____ 319

320 ▪ _____ said that he had the consolation of having added nothing to his private fortune during his public service and of retiring with hands as clean as they were empty.

(a) Thomas Jefferson
(b) Dwight D. Eisenhower
(c) William Howard Taft
(d) Sam Rayburn

_____ **320**

321 ▪ The battle that made Andrew Jackson a national hero— the Battle of New Orleans—

(a) was actually won by the British.
(b) was fought after the War of 1812 was over.
(c) was really no contest: the British gave up without firing more than a shot or two.
(d) turned on information supplied by prostitutes who had spent the previous week in the Redcoat camp.

_____ **321**

322 ▪ At the age of seventy-two in 1919, Alexander Graham Bell (1847–1922)

    (a) posed nude with Mrs. Bell and their seven children for Bernarr Macfadden's magazine *Physical Culture*; thousands of people immediately sold their stock in Bell Telephone.

    (b) set a speed record of seventy miles per hour in a hydrofoil boat of ten thousand pounds.

    (c) joined with Henry Ford, Harvey Firestone and John D. Rockefeller to lobby Congress to outlaw Thomas A. Edison's nonpolluting electric automobile.

    (d) figured out a way to raise the *Titanic*, but the Cunard owners wouldn't let him even try.

_____ **322**

323 ▪ The gigantic painting *Washington Crossing the Delaware* was painted in

    (a) Germany.

    (b) a barge on the Delaware.

    (c) an institution for the blind.

    (d) secret by a slave on a plantation near Mount Vernon.

_____ **323**

324 ▪ _____ believed that the United States could not go to war with Germany and maintain the ideals of government "that all thinking men shared."

    (a) Henry Cabot Lodge, Sr.

    (b) Arthur H. Vandenberg

    (c) Woodrow Wilson

    (d) Cordell Hull

_____ **324**

325 ▪ Through President_____'s administration, it had been a world without ice hockey, the hypodermic needle, the Bunsen burner, Central Park in New York City, *Leaves of Grass*, the flush toilet, the dogma of the Immaculate Conception, baseball rules stipulating weight and ball size, Gauss's idea for informing extraterrestrials that we're here and "The Song of Hiawatha."

    (a) Andrew Jackson
    (b) Millard Fillmore
    (c) James A. Garfield
    (d) Theodore Roosevelt

_____ **325**

326 ▪ President Grover Cleveland (1837–1908) had a secret:

    (a) he believed in resurrection and had a pyramid built in the basement of the White House.
    (b) he was a sometime homosexual.
    (c) he had an operation for cancer of the jaw.
    (d) he didn't vote for himself for president—any of the three times that he ran.

_____ **326**

327 ▪ Only a couple of hours after the half-starved Confederate army had abandoned the city of_____, President Abraham Lincoln, with son Tad in tow, surveyed the city. The receiving crowd at the shore was entirely Negro. One old timer of sixty came forward on his knees: "Bress de Lawd, dere is de great Messiah!" Mr. Lincoln responded, "Don't kneel to me. You must kneel to God only and thank him for your freedom." The city was

   (a) Richmond.
   (b) Petersburg.
   (c) Atlanta.
   (d) Gettysburg.

_____ **327**

328 ▪ Henry Ford (1863–1947), the quintessential in-car-nation of the American Dream, wanted to have a future in his future. He gained international fame by

(a) reducing production costs and automobile prices at the same time that he was raising worker wages from two dollars to five dollars a day.

(b) paying personally for the building of the first fifteen hundred miles of highway in Middle America.

(c) giving a Model T to anyone who could get to Michigan and drive it away.

(d) setting up free driver-training classes in every community in America.

_____ **328**

329 ▪ It occurred to_____that it was silly and wasteful that people should "live so much by candlelight and sleep by sunshine," so he went to bat for daylight saving time in the summer.

(a) Casey Jones

(b) Nat Love

(c) Benjamin Franklin

(d) Chief Crazy Horse

_____ **329**

330 ▪ After her husband was murdered,_____was judged insane by a court and attempted suicide.

(a) Ida McKinley

(b) Jacqueline Bouvier Kennedy

(c) Mary Todd Lincoln

(d) Gladys Garfield

_____ **330**

331 ▪ "My God, what is there in this place that a man would ever want to get into it?"

   (a) James A. Garfield, about the White House
   (b) Lucky Luciano, about New York City
   (c) Robert Redford, about Hollywood
   (d) Diamond Jim Brady, about Delmonico's

_____ **331**

332 ▪ The vice-president announced during a debate in the Senate on national needs that "what the country really needs is a good five-cent cigar," and he was the first vice-president to be reelected in_____years.

   (a) sixty
   (b) nearly a hundred
   (c) thirty
   (d) nearly two hundred

_____ **332**

333 ▪ One man, and one man only, has represented two states in the House of Representatives, and one man, and one man only, has represented three states in the Senate.

   (a) Thaddeus Stevens...Herbert Lehman
   (b) Daniel Webster...Frank Kellogg
   (c) David Wilmont...Alexander James Dallas
   (d) Matthew Lyon...James Shields

_____ **333**

334 ▪ William Lloyd Garrison (1805–1879) was so dedicated to the abolitionist cause that he took offense at

(a) anyone who voted against Abraham Lincoln in the 1864 election.
(b) *Uncle Tom's Cabin*.
(c) Frederick Douglass' plea that women should get the vote before even freed blacks.
(d) the Emancipation Proclamation for not freeing slaves in the North.

_____ **334**

335 ▪ _____wrote about Franklin Roosevelt's presidential aspirations, "Franklin Roosevelt is no crusader. He is no tribune of the people. He is no enemy of entrenched privilege. He is a pleasant man, who, without any important qualifications for office, would very much like to be president."

(a) Arthur Krock
(b) Walter Lippmann
(c) Edward R. Murrow
(d) Joseph Wood Krutch

_____ **335**

336 ▪ The first automobile (literally, "self-moving" on the road) and the first amphibian vehicle (literally a vehicle "living on both" land and water) made their debut in the same year, for they were one and the same.

(a) 1805
(b) 1869
(c) 1889
(d) 1901

_____ 336

337 ▪ When the *New York News* published antiadministration editorials and when the *New York World* two years later satirized the president, the_____administration closed down the papers.

(a) Wilson
(b) Jackson
(c) Lincoln
(d) Truman

_____ 337

338 ▪ So that he might demonstrate his devotion to equality, Congressman Thaddeus Stevens (1792–1868)

(a) lived half of the time in the South and half of the time in the North.
(b) changed his name to Rufus Alice.
(c) ordered that he be buried among blacks in a cemetery in Lancaster, Pennsylvania.
(d) walked around the capital with a blackened face.

_____ 338

339 ▪ Mrs. Elizabeth Seelman Kingsley invented the

    (a) flat iron.
    (b) book club.
    (c) game of Mah-Jongg.
    (d) Double-Crostic.

_____ **339**

340 ▪ The observance of Memorial Day was urged by

    (a) Margaret Mitchell.
    (b) Lucy Hayes.
    (c) John A. Logan.
    (d) the Grimke sisters.

_____ **340**

341 ▪ Senator Joseph McCarthy (1908–1957), who gained notoriety with his reckless anticommunism tactics and smears before being censured by his peers in 1954, completed four years of high school in nine months. He started high school when he was

    (a) twenty years old.
    (b) twenty-two years old.
    (c) nine and a half years old.
    (d) eight years old.

_____ **341**

342 ▪ The world's first ecologist was probably_____of, appropriately, Woodstock, Vermont, who completed writing his "groundbreaking" classic, *Man and Nature, or Physical Geography as Modified by Human Action,* while he was President Abraham Lincoln's minister to Italy.

(a) Henry Adams
(b) Elihu Yale
(c) Charles Perkins Marsh
(d) Charles Goodyear

_____ **342**

343 ▪ In their early journalistic relationship, an editor of Horace Greeley's *New York Tribune* wrote the columnist, "It may perhaps give you pleasure to know that [your articles] are read with satisfaction by a considerable number of persons, and are widely reproduced." The columnist was

(a) the queen of Hawaii.
(b) Walt Whitman.
(c) Karl Marx.
(d) Winston Churchill's father.

_____ **343**

344 ▪ The first United States census was taken in

(a) 1790.
(b) 1820.
(c) 1870.
(d) 1900.

_____ **344**

345 ▪ General John Cadwalader (1742–1786) was a Revolutionary War hero who spent his way to the top of the social heap in Philadelphia by commissioning a lot of expensive furniture that included

(a) the first complete set of Shaker furniture.
(b) chairs, tables and pole screens with hairy feet for his gilded rococo parlors.
(c) one of everything that Thomas Chippendale made.
(d) a duplicate of the boudoir in the home of John Standish and Priscilla Alden.

_____ **345**

346 ▪ Edgar Lee Masters (1869–1950), who may be best remembered for his *Spoon River Anthology*—those poetic small-town profiles in the guise of epitaphs—

(a) deciphered the Japanese naval code in the Second World War.
(b) rewrote his famous poetic work about seventy times.
(c) became Clarence Darrow's law partner.
(d) played third base for the New York Yankees at the turn of the century.

_____ **346**

347 ▪ Philander C. Knox (1853–1921), attorney general under William McKinley and Theodore Roosevelt, and secretary of state under William Howard Taft, was expelled from West Virginia University for a violation of the code of conduct, namely, for

(a) "streaking" during the coed's May Day party.
(b) cheating on a Latin examination.
(c) living up to his given name and philandering with the wife of the university's dean of men.
(d) entering a billiards parlor.

_____ 347

348 ▪ _____ was defeated for the legislature, failed in business, suffered a nervous breakdown, was defeated for nomination for Congress, lost renomination to Congress, was rejected for land office, was defeated for the Senate, was defeated for nomination for vice-president, was defeated for the Senate, became president.

(a) Abraham Lincoln
(b) William McKinley
(c) James Madison
(d) Jimmy Carter

_____ 348

349 ▪ A black man charged with murder was tied to a stake on the stage of an opera house in Livermore, Kentucky, in 1911:

    (a) the location and the price of tickets determined the number of gun shots that the customers were allowed to fire at the prisoner.

    (b) he was starved to death.

    (c) he was allowed to go free when a halo of light mysteriously circumscribed his head.

    (d) he had to recite the Emancipation Proclamation 1863 times without stopping, then was branded "A.L." and released. He dropped dead at the apron of the stage.

_____ 349

350 ▪ The frontier lawman Bat Masterson ended up being

    (a) a sportswriter in New York.

    (b) the third governor of California.

    (c) an ally of Jesse and Frank James.

    (d) bested by Annie Oakley in a winner-take-all rifle contest.

_____ 350

351 ▪ By the turn of the century, America's most distinguished scientist, Simon Newcomb, Ph.D., LL.D., (1835–1909) had just about made a career of

    (a) damning Darwin.

    (b) exhorting educators to load up their faculties with mathematicians and physicists.

    (c) running for the vice-presidency.

    (d) predicting that man could never fly.

_____ 351

352 ▪ Marquis de Lafayette sought escape from _____ when he signed a contract with Silas Deane in 1776 to serve in the American army as a major general.

    (a) appointment as Paris' minister to the Congo
    (b) his role as a wealthy French nobleman
    (c) imprisonment on a trumped-up charge of murder and certain execution
    (d) going into his father's restaurant business

_____ **352**

353 ▪ Vice-President Garret Augustus Hobart's best-remembered public act was

    (a) taking the assassin's bullets aimed at the crippled President-elect Franklin D. Roosevelt, in the back of an open touring car in a park in Florida in early 1933.
    (b) walking into battle at the head of the first all-black squadron fighting for the Union.
    (c) casting the deciding vote in the Senate against granting independence to the Philippines.
    (d) stepping aside in favor of Andrew Johnson at the Republican national convention of 1864.

_____ **353**

354 ▪ When Thomas Edison, "the Wizard of Menlo Park," died on October 18, 1931,

  (a) many Americans observed a voluntary "dim out" as a sign of respect.
  (b) it was not believed by many for a year—"men like Edison never die!"
  (c) he was placed in a casket containing one of everything he had invented—a stock ticker, an electric light bulb, a voting machine, a battery, a phonograph, and so on.
  (d) stock in his company fell overnight from 186¼ to 19.

_____ **354**

355 ▪ "The horses of members of Congress were sometimes turned out into the street," _____ wrote, "because the livery stable keeper was unpaid."

  (a) Molly Pitcher
  (b) Abigail Adams
  (c) Thomas Jefferson
  (d) Betsy Ross

_____ **355**

356 ▪ "Ballads, bons mots, and anecdotes give us better insights into the depths of past centuries than grave and voluminous chronicles," in the opinion of_____

  (a) Bob Dylan.
  (b) Ralph Waldo Emerson.
  (c) Carl Sandburg.
  (d) Arthur Scheslinger.

_____ **356**

357 ▪ The ashes of the legendary union organizer Joe Hill (c.1872–1915) were scattered in every state except one. The exception was the state in which he was killed.

(a) Oregon.
(b) Georgia.
(c) Vermont.
(d) Utah.

_____ **357**

358 ▪ _____'s favorite story was about a druggist in the state of Maine, where they had a prohibition law: No alcoholic liquor could be sold, and an Irishman came in—the word among them for liquor was "the crathur," the creature. And the Irishman asked for a glass of lemonade, and as the druggist was fixing it, he said, "And could you put in a wee bit of the crathur, unbeknownst to me?" And once in a public speech, _____had a sentence: "I am like the Irishman—I have to do some things unbeknownst to myself."

(a) Adlai Stevenson
(b) Al Smith
(c) John F. Kennedy
(d) Abraham Lincoln

_____ **358**

359 ▪ _____translated into English a classic of science, *De re metallica*, published in 1556, whose author, the German mineralologist Georg Agricola, had summarized all the practical knowledge gained by the miners of Saxony.

(a) Dizzy and Paul Dean
(b) Samuel and Mildred Goldwyn
(c) President and Mrs. Herbert Hoover
(d) Theodore Roosevelt

_____ 359

360 ▪ The mansion still standing in the national military cemetery at Arlington, Virginia, just south of the nation's capital, had been the home of

(a) Jefferson Davis.
(b) John Wilkes Booth.
(c) Barbara Fritchie.
(d) Robert E. Lee.

_____ 360

361 ▪ _____presidents haven't vetoed a single bill.

(a) Eight
(b) Fourteen
(c) Twenty-three
(d) Thirty-three

_____ 361

362 ▪ During the First World War this brilliant army staff officer's request for a combat command was refused. In 1933, his job in the army was senior instructor for the Illinois National Guard. In 1939 he was

(a) second in command of the German third armored division that cut off Warsaw from the north.
(b) helping Walt Disney design recruitment cartoon films.
(c) chief of staff of the United States Army.
(d) helping the security forces of United States Steel put down worker riots.

_____ **362**

363 ▪ "Self-pity,"_____ said, "is our worst enemy and if we yield to it, we can never do anything wise in the world."

(a) Franklin D. Roosevelt
(b) Zelda Fitzgerald
(c) Helen Keller
(d) Willie Shoemaker

_____ **363**

364 ▪ After the Civil War the Confederate general George Pickett

(a) was invited to lead the Egyptian army.
(b) revealed that he had intentionally lost the Battle of Gettysburg.
(c) fled to Mexico City to form an army that would take over the southwest United States.
(d) established the *New York Times*.

_____ **364**

155

365 ▪ The New Englander believed that the nation's Anglo-Saxon heritage would be polluted by non-English aliens, yet he favored intervention in Cuba and American overseas expansion. Henry Adams said of him: "Roosevelts are born and never can be taught; but_____was a creature of teaching—Boston incarnate...he could never feel perfectly at ease whatever leg he stood, but shifted, sometimes with painful strain of temper, from one sensitive muscle to another, uncertain whether to pose as an uncompromising Yankee; or a pure American; or a patriot in the still purer atmosphere of Irish, Germans, or Jews; or a scholar and historian of Harvard College. English to the last fibre of his thought—saturated with English literature, English tradition, English taste—revolted by every vice and by most virtues of Frenchmen and Germans, or any other Continental standards, but at home and happy among the vices and extravagances of Shakespeare; he betrayed the consciousness that he and his people had a past, if they dared but avow it, and might have a future, if they could but divine it."

(a) Henry Cabot Lodge Sr.
(b) Oliver Wendell Holmes Sr.
(c) Gore Vidal, Sr.
(d) Louis Brandeis

_____ **365**

366 ▪ Maury Hall at the United States Naval Academy in Annapolis is named in honor of a man who

(a) tried to destroy the United States Navy.
(b) was graduated from West Point.
(c) broke the U-boat code in 1917.
(d) predicted that there could never be such a vessel as an aircraft carrier.

_____ **366**

367 ▪ These four military men were also important figures in _____: John Jay, Robert Harrison, George Clinton and Benjamin Lincoln.

(a) the basketball-betting scandal that broke around the City College of New York thirty years ago
(b) the first presidential election in 1788
(c) the writing of the Emancipation Proclamation
(d) the conspiracy that led to the United States' entry into the Spanish-American War

_____ **367**

368 ▪ He claims to have slept through his presidency, if indeed he was president.

(a) John Peter Mettauer
(b) David Rice Atchison
(c) Calvin Coolidge
(d) John A. Tyler

_____ **368**

369 ▪ In the spring of 1856, pro-slavery forces from Missouri burned the homes of free-staters in Lawrence, Kansas. Revenge was gained by_____and other abolitionists when five pro-slavers were massacred. _____pledged that he would "die fighting for this cause. There will be no peace in this land until slavery is done for. I will give them something else to do than to extend slave territory. I will carry the war into Africa." He was

(a) William Cullen Bryant.
(b) John Brown.
(c) Robert Todd Lincoln.
(d) Ulysses S. Grant.

_____ 369

370 ▪ Some twenty years after striking black gold—petroleum!—in western Pennsylvania, in 1859, Edwin Drake

    (a) was still in his railroad job "because I really like that little red caboose."
    (b) had married some twenty times, keeping each of his erstwhile spouses in the style to which they literally overnight had become accustomed.
    (c) died impecunious.
    (d) was the richest man in America, and one of the richest in the world.

                                   _____ **370**

371 ▪ The first president to visit a foreign country was_____, and he visited_____

    (a) Grover Cleveland...Canada.
    (b) Theodore Roosevelt...Panama.
    (c) Zachary Taylor...Mexico.
    (d) Thomas Jefferson...France.

                                   _____ **371**

372 ▪ Signing of the Declaration of Independence took place over

    (a) a weekend.
    (b) three hours.
    (c) three months.
    (d) half a year.

                                   _____ **372**

373 ▪ General Douglas MacArthur (1880–1964), who had been called upon by President Herbert Hoover in the summer of 1932 to rout the Bonus Army of unemployed veterans in Washington,

(a) wore long hair and dresses when a child.

(b) presently found himself in a Bonus Army being routed by his successor, Dwight D. Eisenhower.

(c) declared "I shall return" when Eleanor Roosevelt asked him to leave the White House after disrupting a dinner party in 1937.

(d) challenged the obdurate President Harry S. Truman to a duel at fifty paces on Wake Island in 1951, prompting the commander in chief to fire him as supreme commander in the Korean war.

_____ **373**

374 ▪ When Harry Burn, a twenty-four-year-old Tennessee legislator, took to heart his mother's exhortation,

(a) the Nineteenth Amendment became the law of the land.

(b) he gave up the law and moved to Minneapolis, where he became "Betty Crocker."

(c) he left on the next boat for Paris and wrote many exceptional novels, including *Finnegans Wake*.

(d) he came out of the closet and revealed that he was a transsexual, causing a furor in the state that faded only in recent years.

_____ **374**

375 ▪ As secretary of state, _____ was the first to devise the twin strategies of "brinkmanship" and "massive retaliation."

    (a) Edwin Stanton
    (b) John Hay
    (c) John Foster Dulles
    (d) Henry Kissinger

_____ 375

376 ▪ _____ presidents were professional soldiers.

    (a) Two
    (b) Six
    (c) Nine
    (d) Twelve

_____ 376

377 ▪ Susanna Haswell Rowson was America's first

    (a) bestselling novelist.
    (b) aviatrix.
    (c) Congressional Medal of Honor winner.
    (d) Miss America beauty contest winner.

_____ 377

378 ▪ On the eve of the Civil War, about _____ blacks themselves owned slaves.

  (a) fifty
  (b) ten or eleven
  (c) two thousand
  (d) a million

_____ **378**

379 ▪ Alexander Hamilton said that "a sacrifice of this sort is entirely repugnant to the genius of the age we live in." And that genius, George Washington, said, "having formed my Opinion upon the most mature reflexion...I can never recede from it." They referred to Washington's decision that

  (a) a British officer should be executed in exemplary retaliation for the murder of a man he had never seen.
  (b) the men and the women and the children—everyone— in Fort Dusquene must be returned to England with their British lovers.
  (c) he would run for a third term as president, though Mrs. Washington had her heart set on their retirement to Mount Vernon.
  (d) the captured Hessians be branded.

_____ **379**

380 ▪ Once the Revolutionary War was over, the new United States of America was a country without

(a) a penny in the bank.
(b) an army, a navy or a marine corps.
(c) a city left unburned.
(d) enough soldiers to head off an invasion by the British army sulking at the Canadian border.

_____ **380**

381 ▪ "You are in honor bound to join hands in favor of law and order and to war against all crime, and especially against all crime by men of your own race, for the heaviest wrong done by the criminal is that wrong to his own race. You must teach the people of your race that they must scrupulously observe any contract into which they in good faith enter, no matter whether it is hard to keep or not. If you save money, secure homes, become taxpayers..." When President Theodore Roosevelt said this, he was addressing

(a) the first convention, in Yorktown, Virginia, of the German Bund.
(b) an all-black student body.
(c) Indian students, from an Oklahoma reservation.
(d) American-born Orientals.

_____ **381**

382 • _____ said, "Our policy is peace and the freest possible trade. Mutual interest should lead to powerful trade . . . but if war is necessary, we will fight for independence."

    (a) Samuel Adams
    (b) Geronimo
    (c) Jefferson Davis
    (d) Frederick Douglass

_____ **382**

383 • After the Wright brothers' historic first four powered flights, a sudden, violent gust of wind upended and severely damaged the aeroplane as it rested on the ground:

    (a) scavengers broke off pieces and sold them to bidders around the world.
    (b) a government official shipped it to Washington for immediate exhibition in the Smithsonian Institution.
    (c) the Wrights dismantled the machine, packed it into two boxes and a barrel and shipped it home to their bicycle shop in Dayton, Ohio.
    (d) the Wrights abandoned it, and the freezingly cold spectators used the pieces for firewood.

_____ **383**

384 • The first presidential press conference was held by

    (a) Thomas Jefferson.
    (b) Theodore Roosevelt.
    (c) Woodrow Wilson.
    (d) Franklin D. Roosevelt.

_____ **384**

385 ■ _____'s earliest vivid memory was of "a frightening confusion of pistol shots and shouting and smoke and flames."

(a) J. Edgar Hoover
(b) Joe Hill
(c) Malcolm X
(d) Clyde Barrow

_____ **385**

386 ■ The first President to visit China was

(a) Theodore Roosevelt.
(b) Franklin Roosevelt.
(c) Richard M. Nixon.
(d) Ulysses S. Grant.

_____ **386**

387 ■ When John Peter Zenger (1697–1746) was editor of the antigovernment paper the *New York Weekly Journal* and was arrested for seditious libel,

(a) the *Journal* had to quit publishing.
(b) Mrs. Zenger took over the editorship and soon found herself in jail for seditious libel.
(c) Zenger was eventually acquitted by the court and his name became linked with the individual's right to discuss and criticize publicly his government and its officers.
(d) Zenger was burned at the stake in lower Manhattan (where the Statue of Liberty now stands), copies of the *Journal* wrapped around his otherwise bare torso.

_____ **387**

165

388 ▪ Only once has the Senate selected the vice-president, and that was in

(a) 1789.
(b) 1824.
(c) 1836.
(d) 1924.

_____ 388

389 ▪ President_____promised that he would retire after one term, and he did.

(a) John Quincy Adams
(b) James K. Polk
(c) Rutherford B. Hayes
(d) Calvin Coolidge

_____ 389

390 ▪ Three years before the Civil War erupted, it took the House of Representatives eight weeks of balloting to

(a) vote the taxes that would raise the level of the army to ten thousand men.
(b) elect a speaker.
(c) agree on the number of slaves that each congressman could have.
(d) fine former President John Tyler for having fathered fifteen children, one of whom was five years older than Mr. Tyler's second wife, Julie Gardiner.

_____ 390

391 ▪ _____ was one vote away from becoming the eighteenth president.

    (a) Edwin Stanton
    (b) Benjamin Wade
    (c) Samuel J. Tilden
    (d) Horace Greeley

_____ **391**

392 ▪ For the last couple decades of his life, the Revolutionary patriot Paul Revere

    (a) wore a uniform of the Revolution.
    (b) gave away at least one complete set of his prized silver every week.
    (c) had an affair (or so he said) with a different Boston matron every day.
    (d) re-enacted his famous (and aborted) ride from Boston to Lexington and Concord.

_____ **392**

393 ▪ When the gold in Fort Knox was last counted in the late 1950s, it totaled $_____

    (a) 30,442,415,581.70.
    (b) 382,673,899,050.07.
    (c) 2,659,440,800.00.
    (d) 434,500,098.00.

_____ **393**

394 ▪ Only one man has presided over both the House of Representatives and the Senate on the same day:

    (a) Daniel Webster.
    (b) Franklin D. Roosevelt.
    (c) Schuyler Colfax.
    (d) John Nance Garner.

_____ **394**

395 ▪ The first black to sit in a president's cabinet was

    (a) Ralph Bunche.
    (b) Paul Robeson.
    (c) Booker T. Washington.
    (d) Robert C. Weaver.

_____ **395**

396 ▪ *"Exitus acta probat"*—the end justifies the means—was the family motto of

    (a) George Washington.
    (b) Geronimo.
    (c) John D. Rockefeller.
    (d) John Dillinger.

_____ **396**

397 ▪ Henry Clay (1777–1852), for more than forty years a public official, delivered an hour-long speech in the Senate about Orozimbo, who was_____

    (a) his dead bull.
    (b) his Indian wife of nearly half a century.
    (c) his black valet for all of his life.
    (d) president of Siam when Clay was President John Quincy Adams' secretary of state.

_____ **397**

398 ▪ In only one year,_____, has the United States not had a national debt.

    (a) 1789
    (b) 1811
    (c) 1835
    (d) 1944

_____ **398**

399 ▪ The only cabinet member to go to jail for misusing his trust has been

    (a) President Warren G. Harding's secretary of the interior.
    (b) President James K. Polk's secretary of manifest destiny.
    (c) President Woodrow Wilson's secretary of human rights.
    (d) President Richard M. Nixon's secretary of dirty tricks.

_____ **399**

400 ▪ Annie Oakley (1860–1926), the Peerless Lady Wing-Shot, capped an outstanding career as markswoman by

(a) shooting a cigarette from the lips of the future Kaiser Wilhelm of Germany.
(b) gunning down Buffalo Bill Cody, "who had done her wrong."
(c) crippling a man intent on assassinating President William Howard Taft with a shot at 330 yards from the outfield scoreboard at a baseball game in Washington, D.C.
(d) offering to donate her eyes to Helen Keller.

_____ **400**

401 ▪ The first president to be inaugurated in January, rather than in March, was_____

(a) Thomas Jefferson.
(b) Grover Cleveland (first term).
(c) Franklin D. Roosevelt (second term).
(d) Dwight D. Eisenhower (second term).

_____ **401**

402 ∙ Being the most powerful man in the nation, sometimes in the world—being president of the United States—does not guarantee reelection. _____ presidents have been defeated in reelection bids by their political party or by the voters.

(a) Two
(b) Seven
(c) Ten
(d) Eleven

_____ **402**

403 ∙ _____ said, "I feel myself eased of a load of public care. I hope to spend the remainder of my days in cultivating the affections of good men, and in the practice of the domestic virtues."

(a) Omar Bradley
(b) George Washington
(c) Dwight D. Eisenhower
(d) Douglas MacArthur

_____ **403**

■ ANSWERS ON PAGE 251

404 ▪

> America, thou hast it better
> Than our old continent; ...
> Within, naught restrains thee
> From a livelier era;
> No useless memories
> Of unforgotten strife
> Face thy future with happiness.

The poet was
(a) Shakespeare.
(b) Goethe.
(c) Wordsworth.
(d) Laotze.

_____ **404**

Answers

1 (b) From the sixteenth president's second message to Congress, December 1, 1862; the Civil War was raging.

2 (a) British Prime Minister Churchill (1874–1965) has been celebrated as "the Man of the Century," "the terrible twentieth," Sir Winston himself called it. Wallenberg, a Lutheran banker (1912–?) served—at the behest of the United States War Refugee Board and the World Jewish Congress—with the neutral Swedish legation in Nazi-occupied Budapest, where he helped to save the lives of more than one hundred thousand Jews in the last year of the Second World War. He was taken into "protective custody" by liberating Russian troops and hasn't been seen or heard from since.

3 (a) The design, supported by John Adams and Thomas Jefferson, was rejected by the Continental Congress. When the bald eagle was selected six years later as the national symbol, Franklin wrote that the eagle is a "bird of bad moral character," living by "sharping and robbing." He then proposed that the turkey be the symbol.

4 (c) "The Court finds the first charge against Lieu't Colo Paul Revere to be supported (to wit) his refusing to deliver a certain Boat to the Order of General Wadsworth when upon the Retreat up Penobscot River from Major Bagwaduce: but the Court taking into consideration the suddenness of the refusal, and more especially that the same Boat was in fact employed by Lieu't Colo Paul Revere to effect the Purpose ordered by the General as appears by the General's Deposition, are of the Opinion that Lieu't Colo Paul Revere be acquitted of this Charge. On the second charge, the Court considers that the whole army was in great Confusion and so scattered and dispersed, that no regular Orders were or could be given, are of the Opinion, that Lieu't Colo Paul Revere, be acquitted with equal Honor as the other Officers in the same Expedition."

5 (a) By the margin of one vote, President Lincoln's second vice-president and successor was saved in May 1868 from congressional conviction for his Reconstruction ("malice toward none") policies—his reputation for honesty proved invaluable and he had been the only Southern senator to oppose secession. After

QUESTIONS ON PAGE 7 ■

leaving the White House, Johnson (1808–1875) lost a Senate campaign in his native Tennessee, then a House campaign, then won a Senate seat. He died four months after returning to Capitol Hill.

6 (b) A bomb exploded and rioting ensued in Haymarket Square in Chicago, in May 1886, killing seven policemen and injuring 100 persons. Though no evidence was produced that they had made or thrown the bomb, eight anarchists were tried and convicted of inciting violence; four were hanged and one committed suicide; the remaining three were pardoned (after being imprisoned for seven years) on grounds that the trial had been unjust. Before the trap was sprung, the condemned August Spies said, "You may strangle this voice but my silence will be more terrible than speech."

7 (d) Though inept he refused to resign. Hancock (1737–1793) was bitterly disappointed when Washington, and not he, became commander in chief of the Continental Army. He was elected governor of Massachusetts nine times, dying of gout in office.

8 (d) "Whereas Lieutenant General George Washington of Virginia commanded our armies throughout and to the successful termination of our Revolutionary War; Whereas Lieutenant General George Washington presided over the convention that formulated our Constitution; Whereas Lieutenant General George Washington twice served as President of the United States of America; and Whereas it is considered fitting and proper that no officer of the United States should outrank Lieutenant General George Washington on the Army list: Now, therefore, be it Resolved by the Senate and the House of Representatives of the United States of America in Congress assembled, That (a) for purposes of subsection (b) of this section only, the grade of General of the Armies of the United States is established, such grade to have rank and precedence over all other grades of the Army, past or present. (b) The President is authorized and requested to appoint George Washington posthumously to the grade of General of the Armies of the United States, such appointment to take effect on July 4, 1976. Approved October 11, 1976." Washington was appointed General of the Army by the Continental Congress on June 15, 1775, and held that commission until December 23,

1783, when he resigned it. In 1798, after the adoption of the Constitution, Congress passed a law authorizing the president to raise a provisional army. Among the provisions of that act, section 5 authorized the rank of lieutenant general for the commander of the armies of the United States. Washington was commissioned in that rank on July 3, 1798, and held it until his death a year later.

9 (a) TR (1858–1919) considered the inscription unconstitutional and sacrilegious. "In God We Trust" did not appear on a U.S. coin until 1864.

10 (a) Existing arrangements seemed very poor to the legendary musical innovator, so he produced a unique version of the national anthem, with seventh chords added to the familiar harmonies. Before a second performance in Boston, in the winter of 1944, a police commissioner appeared in the maestro's dressing room and informed him of a state law forbidding any tampering with national property; policemen, in fact, were instructed to remove Stravinsky's arrangement from the music stands. Stravinsky argued that "if an Urtext of the 'Star-spangled Banner' existed, it was certainly infrequently played in Massachusetts," but to no avail. Later, Stravinsky wrote that his version really ought to be performed, "for it makes the linear and harmonic best of the material, and is certainly superior to any other version I have heard. (The compliment to myself in this comparison is very small indeed.)"

11 (c) On the day that Jefferson died, July 4, 1826, dead broke and in debt, friends were soliciting money for his relief in the House of Representatives at a ceremony marking the fiftieth anniversary of the Declaration of Independence.

12 (b) She returned to her native Germany, was arrested by the Nazis as a "useless person"—not only was she a midget, she was half Jewish—and shipped to the death camp.

13 (c) Amortizing slavery would be vastly preferable to a war, and in Lincoln's plan the borrowed money would not have to be liquidated until the 1910s. The president's stroke of genius and profound political resourcefulness were thought to be merely a political gimmick, and that was the end of that idea.

14 (c) 1971.

15 (a) The bell was hanging in the Philadelphia statehouse, but no one thought of ringing it. Nor did it have a sobriquet. Fifty-two years later, in 1828, the city tried to sell the bell as scrap but could find no buyers: the bell was not worth the expense of removing it from the building. In 1839, it was referred to for the first time as the Liberty Bell—in a pamphlet entitled "The Liberty Bell, by Friends of Freedom," distributed at the Massachusetts Anti-Slavery Fair, and the bell symbolized the freedom of black slaves, not the independence of white Americans from Britain. In 1847 a Philadelphia journalist, George Lippard (1822–1854), invented the story about the bell having been rung in celebration of the colonies' independence.

16 (c) Kemmler was put to death on August 6, 1890. In all, the state of New York has killed 695 prisoners in "Sparky." (Three brothers were executed on the same day in 1903.) Before the electric chair, at least 400 criminals in New York were executed by a variety of methods, including being burned at the stake.

17 (b) Maryland legislator Thomas Kennedy, a Catholic, declared in the 1820s, "I know no Jews, but they deserve to hold public office like the rest of us." (Some colonists on arrival in the New World believed that the Indians were descendants of the lost tribes of Israel. The first recorded Jews arrived in America in 1624—two men and one woman disembarked in Virginia. On the eve of the Revolution, there were about fifteen hundred Jews living in the colonies.)

18 (d) Georgia, Massachusetts and Connecticut ratified the Bill of Rights after one hundred and fifty years. The bill had become law by the margin of exactly one vote in 1791; approval of three-quarters of the fourteen states was needed, and only the eleven necessary votes were obtained.

19 (c) The prolific composer (over three thousand songs) decided, however, that "God Bless America" wasn't appropriate for the Ziegfeld Follies, so he withheld it from public performance for many years until Armistice Day, 1938. Kate Smith introduced what became a patriotic masterpiece, and she sang it thousands of times. Royalties are divided by Mr. Berlin between the Boy Scouts and the Girl Scouts. (Mr. Berlin's most popular composition is "White Christmas"—more than 150 million records and copies of the sheet music have been bought.)

20 (d) "I burned a PRO-SLAVERY Constitution, in my judgment," Garrison was to write responding to criticism, "in the judgment of the nation ever since its adoption, and therefore was faithful to the slave in so doing; and not one of his 'sincere and true friends' will ever reproach me for the deed—the light of which shall be seen long after this mortal shall have put on immortality." Garrison ceased publication of his abolitionist newspaper, the *Liberator*, when the Civil War was over and slavery was dead, and became president of the Free Trade League, arguing for prohibition, fair treatment of Indians and women's suffrage.

21 (a) Ward refused to kowtow—which the Chinese emperor had demanded—or even touch the floor with one knee. But the emperor was informed that since Americans were "socially backward," how could Mr. Ward comprehend the niceties of diplomacy? When a treaty was arranged, it could not be signed in Peking because Mr. Ward would have had to get down on his knees three times and knock his forehead on the floor or ground thrice at each kneeling—in other words, kowtow.

22 (a) Mary Todd Lincoln's brother, George, a surgeon in the army, is said to have called Lincoln "one of the greatest scoundrels unhung." Mrs. Lincoln's three half brothers were killed fighting for the Confederacy, as was the husband of her half sister, Emilie. (During the war, rumors that Mrs. Lincoln was spying for the Confederacy were abroad in the nation's capital. The president made an unscheduled appearance before the Senate Committee on the Conduct of the War and said, "I, Abraham Lincoln, president of the United States, appear of my own volition before this committee to say that I, of my own knowledge, know it is untrue that any member of my family holds treasonable communication with the enemy"—and that ended that.)

23 (b) The White House was designated "the Palace" in the original plans, which were designed by James Hoban on a site chosen by George Washington. It is the oldest public building in Washington, its cornerstone having been laid in 1792. Our second president, John Adams, moved in during construction. During the War of 1812 the leader of the British expeditionary force occupying Washington polled officers and men assembled in the House of Representatives; they voted to "light up" the capital, and they indeed did. In 1818 President James Monroe had the executive mansion restored and the scorch marks on the smoke-stained gray walls painted white, but sometime between excavation and restoration the cognomen "White House" had been applied to it.

24 (c) Minuit (c. 1580–1638) went on to settle New Sweden, near Trenton, and build Fort Christina, at Wilmington, for a Swedish company. He drowned during a trading expedition to the West Indies.

25 (b) In breaking the century-old precedent, on April 8, 1913, during his first year in office, Mr. Wilson (1856–1924) announced to the Congress that he would use both the muscle of the chief executive and the sinews of the Democratic party chief to lead legislative efforts.

26 (a) In the last years of the sixteenth century, the first theatrical performance was put on in North America, near present-day El Paso. It was a Spanish *comedia* dealing with an expedition of soldiers. In the 1570s, Sir Francis Drake had claimed a slice of California, dubbing it "New England," for Queen Elizabeth I.

27 (d) The Union's surrogate commander, Doubleday had sent word that he would surrender the besieged fort when the food supply was exhausted two days hence. The Confederates' response was to open fire and gain a bloodless victory. (Doubleday's first round "bounded off from the sloping roof of the [ironclad] battery opposite without producing any apparent effect.") The northern garrison was shipped back to New York and Doubleday served gallantly throughout the rest of the war, fighting at Antietam, at Fredericksburg, at Chancellorsville and at Gettysburg. (Credit for inventing baseball as we know it can be given to Alexander J. Cartwright (1820–1892), a surveyor and amateur athlete. The first game played under his rules was staged at Hoboken, New Jersey, on June 19, 1846.)

28 (d) Once a heroine, representative of all the best of American democracy, "Saint Jane" was hysterically transformed into a villain and a traitor because of her activities in the world peace movement and her opposition to the First World War. Pacifists had become synonymous with Reds, and every criticism of the war was interpreted by isolationist superpatriots as un-American and disloyal. She was expelled from the Daughters of the American Revolution. After being passed over year after year for a decade, Miss Addams was honored for promoting peace by the Nobel committee in 1931, but incongruously had to share the prize with a conservative internationalist who had supported America's participation in "the war to end all wars," Nicholas Murray Butler, president of Columbia University for more than forty years.

29 (b) The legendary hero of the Italian Risorgimento, who had worked in a candle factory in Staten Island before conquering Sicily and Naples and installing King Victor Emmanuel, was invited by letter, in June 1861, by the American consul to Antwerp, James Quiggle, to return to the United States and become a Union general. If he were invited directly by the president, Garibaldi responded, he would be happy to help. As Confederate troops made progress—Bull Run was a major triumph for the South—Secretary of State William Seward dispatched an American diplomat, H. S. Sanford, with an invitation to Garibaldi to command an army. His services were "earnestly desired and invited," and he would receive a major general's commission. Garibaldi now said that he would accept if he could also be commander in chief and given the capacity to declare the abolition of slavery—abolition would declare the true significance of the struggle. The conditions could not be met. The Constitution specifically said that the president was commander in chief, and emancipation was not yet part of Lincoln's plan. On September 18, 1861, the American minister to Italy wrote Secretary Seward, ". . . do not believe he [Garibaldi] will take any part in the struggle, unless he is convinced that the Government and the people of the North are united in the determination to pursue a policy which shall necessarily result in the abolition of slavery." Negotiations with Garibaldi resumed in 1862, but to no avail. He was seriously wounded and arrested in an attack on Rome; on October 7, 1862, having been granted amnesty, he made it known to United States Minister George Perkins Marsh that he would gladly serve the United States when he was recovered. By now Ulysses S. Grant was generaling the

Union armies and impressive successes were being scored. Garibaldi's help was no longer needed "in defense of that people which is so dear to me."

30 (b) It is merely a myth that Betsy Ross (1752–1836) was involved in any way in the creation of Old Glory. It was designed by Francis Hopkinson, a lawyer, the first native American composer and a signatory to the Declaration of Independence. The Continental Congress' resolution creating the flag (1777) called for thirteen red and white stripes, but whether they should run horizontally or vertically or both ways was not indicated. After Vermont and Kentucky joined the Union, Congress (on May 1, 1795) adopted a flag of fifteen stars and fifteen stripes. In 1818 it voted to indicate the admission of new states by the addition of stars only, and to revert to a flag of thirteen stripes.

31 (a) Scopes never gave the lecture on evolution. The day that his class reached that part of the book, an athletic event kept him from teaching. Pupils who testified against him in court had to be crammed by the prosecution on what evolution even was. The jury's verdict of guilty was upset on a technicality and Scopes was let go. When the case went on appeal before the Tennessee Supreme Court, Scopes was so engrossed in his studies of geology at the University of Chicago (where grateful scientists had established a scholarship for him) that he did not bother to return to the state. The higher court reversed the decision that Scopes be fined one hundred dollars. The Tennessee law that Scopes challenged was not repealed until forty years after the trial.

32 (c) Service on the 1,966-mile route between St. Joseph, Missouri, and Sacramento, California, was curtailed by Indian raids, and the new transcontinental telegraph did it in once and for all in late 1861.

33 (d) The Irish-born Vermonter (1750–1822), a political Jeffersonian, and once an indentured servant and "a Green Mountain Boy," had attacked President John Adams' plainly unconstitutional Sedition Act, which forebade defamation of the government or its officers or to bring them into contempt or disrepute. The act, negating the free speech and the free press amendments to the Constitution, was repealed during the succeeding Jefferson administration after seventy men had been jailed and fined. James Madison said the act was "a monster and must forever disgrace its parents." By an informal decision it was declared unconstitutional by the Supreme Court—in 1964.

34 (b) Orville sold the American Wright Co. in 1914 and devoted his life to airplane research. He died in 1948, thirty-six years after Wilbur.

35 (b) From the sounds of the forest and his people, the silver craftsman and warrior (c. 1770–1843) knew that feelings and passions were conveyed by different sounds, and when he had distinguished the sounds, he attempted to convey them through pictorial signs—images of birds and beasts. He then made the cultural leap from hierogylphics to syllabaries, reducing the number of characters in his alphabet to eighty-one. The Cherokee proved to be quick learners because the syllabary was simple and its adoption to speech and thought was easy, and almost all the nation was made literate. He determined to seek out other tribes of Indians whose representatives he had met on a journey to Washington in 1828 so that they might help to initiate his project of pan-Indian literacy. He died on his trip South seeking Cherokee who had wandered toward Mexico, and his greater vision was never realized.

36 (c) The philanthropic Carnegie, the steel magnate (1835–1919), donated a lake to Princeton University, in the early 1900s: "Princeton should have a rowing crew to compete with Harvard, Yale, and Columbia. That will take young men's minds off football ... I have never seen a football game, but I have glanced at pictures of such games, and to me the spectacle of educated young men rolling over one another in the dirt was—well, not gentlemanly ... the maimed and the killed are not the worst feature, it is the trickery, fraud, etc., the plot to concentrate and disable certain players on the other side, etc., that make the game so objectionable." The cost of the lake, three and one half miles long, four hundred to one thousand feet wide, was $400,000.

37 (a) Napoleon (1769–1821) died before the rescue expedition could be mounted. Girod, a stanch Frenchman and a great philanthropist, had erected and furnished a house at 124 Chartres

183

Street, near St. Louis Street, for Napoleon's use; it is known today as The Napoleon House.

38 (b) After the war the Wales native was sent by the *New York Herald* to find the missionary David Livingstone, who had gone into the interior of Africa in 1866 to seek the source of the Nile. Stanley, after great travail, found Livingstone at Ujiji, a village on the eastern shore of Lake Tanganyika. Later he ascertained that Lake Victoria was a single body of water, and he traced the Congo River.

39 (b) Lewis (1885–1951) became in 1930 the first American to win the Nobel Prize for Literature, which he accepted.

40 (a) The implacable Henry "Light-Horse Harry" Lee (1756–1818) fought with distinction in many campaigns and participated in the siege of Yorktown that essentially ended the Revolution. He wrote the most famous eulogy in American history, hailing George Washington as "first in war, first in peace, and first in the hearts of his countrymen." The two Lees are interred in Lexington, Virginia, the site of Washington and Lee University.

41 (c) The first director of the Smithsonian Institution headed the nation's scientific mobilization during the Civil War.

42 (c) Major General Taylor (1784–1850) died sixteen months after being sworn in, leaving as his administration's signal achievement the Clayton-Bulwer Treaty with England, providing for joint control of any canal built across the Central American isthmus.

43 (c) Red Emma (1869–1940), after being released, expressed sympathy with the assassin's motives but offered to nurse the dying McKinley—he was, she said, "a human being." When she was deported in 1919, she said, "We expect to be called back to Soviet America."

44 (b) The Frenchman Alexis de Tocqueville (1805-1859), also had a word or two to say: [about General Jackson]... "whom the Americans have twice elected to be the head of their government, is a man of violent temper and very moderate talents; nothing in his whole career ever proved him qualified to govern a free people; and, indeed, the majority of the enlightened classes of the Union has always opposed him. But he was raised to the Presidency, and has been maintained there solely by the recollection of a victory that he gained, twenty years ago, under the walls of New Orleans, a victory which was, however, a very ordinary achievement and which could only be remembered in a country where battles are rare. Now the people who are thus carried away by the illusions of glory are unquestionably the most cold and calculating, the most unmilitary, if I may so speak, and the most prosaic of all the nations of the earth."

45 (c) The judge (1652–1730) spent a day a year in fasting and prayer—repentance—through the last thirty-three years of his life, accepting "blame and shame" for the verdict. Recent research has suggested that the "witches" had suffered hallucinations after having eaten contaminated bread.

46 (d) They all first occurred during Warren G. Harding's presidency (1921–1923).

47 (a) The first woman member of the House (1916, four years before women got the franchise), the Montanan was twice elected, and coincidentally both times a declaration of war came before the legislative body. Miss Rankin (1880–1973) was the only one in congress to vote against entry into the Second World War. In 1968 she led the Jeannette Rankin Brigade of five thousand women in a march on Capitol Hill to protest U.S. involvement in the Vietnam war.

48 (b) Dr. Charles Richard Drew (1904–1950), a graduate of Amherst, McGill and Columbia, a pioneer in blood-plasma research and a surgical consultant to the army, was black, and his own donation could have been refused outright or used only to aid black servicemen. For supervising New York's blood donations to bombed Britain and for his Red Cross work, he won the 1943 Spingarn Award "for the highest achievement by an American Negro." He died in an automobile crash but, contrary to myth, not because the nearby hospital in North Carolina refused to admit him for a blood transfusion because he was black, Drew's neck had been broken and his chest crushed, and even heroic efforts could not have saved him.

185

49 (c) As summarized by Charles Alperin in *Midstream* in 1979, the substantial quantity of evidence shows that Columbus changed his surname three times during the Inquisition, returning at the beginning of his fame to his ancestral name of Colón, a name held by many Jewish families; in his writings he consistently returned to mentioning the Jews in one way or another, and he constantly compared himself to heroes of the Old Testament; he was deeply interested in Jewish mysticism and had a mystical signature that seems to recall Jewish doctrine; the departure of his first voyage was delayed for one day, which happened to be Tishah-b'Ab, a day of Jewish mourning, when Jews traditionally will not commence a new venture; and in his will there were acts of charity that were Jewish in nature. Brother Nectario M. (a Venezuelan Roman Catholic friar and member-historian of six historical academies) told the Royal Hispano-American Academy in 1966 that Columbus ". . . was a member of a Jewish family of so-called 'Conversos' . . . The proofs that [he] was of Jewish origin are innumerable."

50 (a) Oscar Wilde and Walt Whitman spent nearly the entire afternoon of January 18, 1882, together in Whitman's retirement home. They drank a bottle of wine and proceeded upstairs on a thee and thou basis. Laying a hand on the poet's knee, Wilde (1854–1900) said, "I can't listen to anyone unless he attracts me by a charming style or by beauty of theme." Whitman (1819–1892), stroking his silvery beard, later said, "Wilde seemed to me like a great big splendid boy."

51 (c) John Tyler, Millard Fillmore, Andrew Johnson, James A. Garfield, Theodore Roosevelt, Calvin Coolidge, Harry S. Truman, Lyndon B. Johnson and Gerald R. Ford. (The office of vice-president has been vacant for a combined total of almost thirty-eight years.)

52 (b) During the last thirteen months of the war, Captain Henry Wirz was commander of the notorious Andersonville Prison in Georgia when nearly 14,000 Union men died there. He was hanged seven months after Appomattox. (Four of the conspirators in the plot that killed President Abraham Lincoln were also hanged.) Of the 270,000 captured Union troops in Confederate prisons, 22,576 died, according to Secretary of War Edwin Stanton;

186

there were 26,436 dead among the 220,000 men in Union prisons.

53 (a) The cold-hearted Mary Washington, probably a Tory at heart, deprecated George's achievements and chose not to attend his inaugurations. He had to point out angrily what a drain on his estate her activities had been—during the war he had advanced her between three hundred and four hundred pounds from his own pocket. Still, she talked in such a way that he was "viewed as a delinquent and considered, perhaps by the world, an unjust and undutiful son." President John F. Kennedy's lumpen assassin, Lee Oswald, lived near his mother but they did not speak with each other in the fourteen months before the assassination.

54 (a) The naval hero (1747–1792) had killed a mutinous crew member in self-defense. Many years later he fled Russia when he was falsely accused of raping a young girl in St. Petersburg. He had been born John Paul and assumed the surname Jones in the colonies.

55 (d) Congress had rejected a request for $100,000, and the nation's richest families expressed little interest. The statue was to have been erected during the centennial year of American independence, but it wasn't finished until 1884. Pulitzer's paper editorialized, "The two hundred and fifty thousand dollars that the making of the statue cost was paid in by the masses of the French people—by the working men, the tradesmen, the shopgirls, the artisans—by all, irrespective of class or condition. Let us respond in like manner. Let us not wait for the millionaires to give the money . . . take this appeal to yourself personally. It is meant for every reader of *The World*. Give something, however little. Send it to us. We will receive it, and see that it is properly applied. We will also publish the name of every giver, however small the sum given. Let us hear from the people." One hundred thousand dollars was forthcoming. The French sculptor Frederic Auguste Bartholdi (1834–1904) supervised construction of the base and placement of the statue. Great festivities accompanied the unveiling—and to this day the statue carries the torch for freedom and liberty.

56 (c) He then jilted Mrs. Eaton and eloped with her granddaughter.

57 (a) 1798.

58 (b) The tenth president (1790–1862) served for a brief period in the House of Representatives of the Confederacy. He died a year after the War Between the States started.

59 (c) The poet (1807–1882), long a professor of modern languages and belles lettres, wrote it for his children on a day when little Edith did not want to have her hair curled. (His epic poem *The Song of Hiawatha* was written in the meter of the Finnish epic *Kalevala*.)

60 (d) A European-educated Marxist, DuBois (1868–1963) said that capitalism itself was largely responsible for oppression of the blacks and for the racism that helped to maintain the system. ("To the real question, How does it feel to be a problem?, I answer seldom a word.")

61 (d) Because liquor, as well as tobacco and profanity, was banished from the White House, Mrs. Hayes was also known as "Lemonade Lucy." At one official dinner, the water flowed like champagne.

62 (c) And the Führer kept a framed photograph of Mr. Ford on *his* desk. (Hitler had incorporated into *Mein Kampf* some of Ford's anti-Semitic views and always welcomed Ford's substantial contributions to the Nazi cause. The Reich Youth Leader Baldur von Schirach, whose mother was an American and one of whose great-grandfathers was a Union officer who lost a leg at Bull Run during the U.S. Civil War, told his American jailers at Nuremberg that he had become an anti-Semite at the age of seventeen after reading the book *Eternal Jew*, by Henry Ford.)

63 (b) Should it be British merchants and landowners or American merchants and landowners?

64 (a) Our eighth president (and Andrew Jackson's second vice-president) was born in New York in Kinderhook in 1782 and inaugurated in 1837. The first seven presidents were, of course, born in English colonies.

65 (d) When President Truman's widow died in 1982, America had been spanned from the first president, George Washington, to the incumbent, Ronald Reagan, by only three generations of the families of *two* presidents.

66 (a) But they were "allowed" to break their picks mining and rail-roading and farming and fishing in the American West, contributing to industrial growth. They drained the tule swamps of central California, creating some of the richest farmland in the world.

67 (d) The physicist (1904–1967), the father of the atomic bomb, was describing his ivory-tower life up to late 1936.

68 (c) By a special act of Congress, the former representative (North Carolina, 1811–1816) and senator (Alabama, 1819–1844, 1848–1852) took the oath in Havana as President Franklin Pierce's vice-president. King (1786–1853) died a month later, before the first session of the thirty-third Congress was held, and so never got to preside over the Senate, the vice-president's principal role at the time.

69 (a) The wealthy bachelor (1741–1868) and serious drinker had been told on the eve of the South's secession that he was sleeping on a volcano, that the ground was mined all around him and ready to explode. His proposed constitutional amendments which protected slavery in the South as a solution to the crisis would have been no solution at all.

70 (c) The state legislatures nominated the candidates and less than 5 percent of the electorate participated in the voting. When none of the four candidates received an electoral majority, the decision fell to the House of Representatives. John Quincy Adams (President Monroe's secretary of state) became our sixth president in 1825 "by a fluke," one ballot by an anguished New York State delegate. The historian Paul F. Boller, Jr., has observed that the American people "were lukewarm to [Adams] one of the most intelligent, courageous, experienced, and public-spirited of all our Presidents." Adams, "Old Man Eloquent," after losing his reelection bid, served Massachusetts seventeen years in the House: "No election or appointment conferred upon me ever gave me so much pleasure."

71 (c) The treaty of Guadalupe Hidalgo in 1848 brought into the nation a vast area of the present Southwest from Texas to California

189

and included most of what is now Colorado, Utah, Nevada, New Mexico and Arizona. The United States paid $15 million to Mexico for the territory. The treaty was negotiated by Nicholas Trist (1800–1874), who had studied the law with former President Thomas Jefferson and was his part-time secretary, riding and walking companion and confidant. He was at Jefferson's side when the elder statesman died on July 4, 1826.

72 (b) The only man to run for the White House from behind prison bars received 3.5 percent of the total number of votes cast. He had been jailed under the Espionage Law for speaking out against U.S. entry into the war. In the third year of a ten-year sentence he was freed by President Warren G. Harding in 1921, and the president invited Debs to Washington for a friendly chat. The high-minded Debs ran five times in all for the presidency. He had served seven years in the Indiana legislature.

73 (c) The South apparently planned to stop fighting when its complete independence was acknowledged.

74 (b) Incidentally, the physicist's dying words in 1955 will never be known; his attending nurse did not understand German.

75 (d) Tammany's Boss Tweed (1823–1878), who was bilking New York of tens of millions of dollars, tried to get Nast to call off his visual attacks and go abroad to study art. Tweed did not so much mind what the papers printed about him, he said, because most of his constituents couldn't read, but they damn well could see "them damn pictures." Nast's mordant cartoons helped to seal Tweed's doom. Nast also created the symbols of the Democratic (donkey) and Republican (elephant) parties, and the jolly figure of Santa Claus that we know today.

76 (a) The diagnosis, confirmed by an autopsy, was made by Dr. James B. Herrick (1861–1954) without the benefit of electrocardiograms, blood tests and other sophisticated medical tools now routinely used in cardiology. Doctors were slow to accept the new condition, and the case report, Dr. Herrick was to recall, "fell like a dud." That first patient, a fifty-five-year-old banker, survived for fifty-two hours.

77 (d) In 1784 before the Father of Our Country (1732–1799) became our first president.

190

78 (c) The five-star general and thirty-third president (1890–1969) also said in 1949, "If all that Americans want is security, then they can go to prison. They'll have enough to eat, a bed and a roof over their heads. But if an American wants to preserve his dignity and his equality as a human being, he must not bow his neck to any dictatorial government."

79 (b) It was the first and only time that someone other than the commander in chief has issued a declaration of war against another nation. Since the Treaty of Paris in 1783, there had been border claims by both Maine and New Brunswick (Canada) in Aroostook territory. When the Maine land agent authorized to break up British lumbering camps was arrested by British authorities in 1839, Governor John Fairfield of Maine declared hostilities and mobilized the state militia. New Brunswick called up its militia as well and war preparations were begun by the Nova Scotia legislature. Congress countered, authorizing a force of 50,000 men and $10 million for possible conflict. Bloodshed was averted when President Martin Van Buren sent General Winfield Scott to arrange a truce and the British government agreed to refer the dispute to a boundary commission. The Webster-Ashburton Treaty fixed the present border.

80 (a) The Equal Rights candidate campaigned seriously in 1884 (claiming all of Indiana's electoral votes) and in 1888. Though women were prohibited from voting, Mrs. Lockwood had asked, while supporting the Democratic candidate, Horace Greeley, in 1872, "Why not nominate women for important places? Is not Victoria empress of India? Have we not among our countrywomen persons of as much talent and ability? Is not history full of precedents of women rulers?" Planks of her platform called for equality and justice to all, regardless of color, sex and nationality; pensions for soldiers; equal voting; property rights for women; an end to liquor traffic; and an end of corruption "in high places." When she had finished her courses at National University Law School in the District of Columbia, she was told that she could not be given a diploma because of her gender. When she protested by letter to President Ulysses S. Grant, *ex officio* president of the school, she got her diploma—signed by Grant himself—and was admitted to the District bar that had at first objected. Her daughter reported what happened when

191

Mrs. Lockwood introduced, in 1880, the first Southern Negro to practice before the Supreme Court: "Quite a ripple of excitement was raised in the United States Supreme Court when Mrs. Lockwood proposed the admission of Samuel Lowry, colored, of Alabama, to its bar. Reporters were on the qui vive when the pair entered the Court. Samuel is the first colored man from the South, and the fourth of his race who has been admitted to Court. Some strange fatality has caused all to die but one, and even his obituary has been written. It was suggested if Lowry be told this fact it might deter him, but no one enlightened him."

81 (b) The only president to sit on the high bench was appointed in 1921 by President Warren G. Harding. Ill health forced his resignation nine years later, a month before he died.

82 (c) The Vermonters, led by Ethan Allen (1738–1789), sought to control their land themselves rather than submit to the jurisdiction of others. Two years after Vermont achieved statehood, in 1791, and under the tax laws, the Allen families lost all of their land.

83 (d) Until the Articles of Confederation were ratified in 1781, the nation was known as "The Congress." Under the Articles, it was called "The United States in Congress Assembled." Under the present Constitution, it is called the "United States of America." Paine (1737–1809), said by a contemporary to have been "loathsome in his appearance, and a disgusting egotist," wrote to Congress after the Revolutionary War, "Trade I do not understand. Land I have none . . . I have exiled myself from one country without making a home of another; and I cannot help sometimes asking myself, what am I better off than a refugee." He was given a farm by New York in New Rochelle.

84 (c) Scott (c.1795–1858) had been a slave and a servant in Virginia, Missouri, Illinois (where slavery had been forbidden by the Ordinance of 1787) and the Wisconsin territory (where slavery was prohibited by the Missouri Compromise). In 1846 he sought liberty for himself and his family—his suit (instituted by a white man) was based on the fact that he had lived and traveled on free soil with the consent of his master and therefore was legally free upon his return to Missouri. A lower court's judgment in

Scott's favor was overruled in 1852 by the state supreme court, which previously had ruled that under similar circumstances a slave became free upon his return to Missouri. A majority of the U.S. Supreme Court finally held that Scott (and hence all black slaves or their descendants) was not a citizen of the United States or the state of Missouri and thus was not entitled to sue in federal courts: Scott's temporary residence in free territory had not made him free upon his return to Missouri, and the Missouri Compromise, an act of Congress, was unconstitutional (a ruling made with the hope of preventing similar suits and North-South strife). Northern denunciation of the decision included charges of "conspiracy." (Frederick Douglass, the black leader, was not depressed. "My hopes were never brighter than now. The Supreme Court is not the only power in the world.") While working at Theron Barnum's Hotel in St. Louis, Scott had his portrait painted and the whole Scott family was persuaded to have its picture taken for *Frank Leslie's Illustrated Newspaper*. When Scott died of rapid consumption in St. Louis, a year after being manumitted by Taylor Blow, the funeral expenses were met by one of his previous owners.

85 (a) In 1900 Chapman (1864–1945), the naturalist-editor of *Bird Lore* (the forerunner of *Audubon*), enticed twenty-seven observers to spend "a portion of Christmas Day with the birds and send a report of the hunt before retiring for the night." Today, some thirty-five thousand "birders" spend Christmas scanning forests and fields and recording their findings. The sponsoring National Audubon Society says that it is one of the few research operations in which amateurs can make contributions valuable to scientists.

86 (d) The pupils were inspired by Oliver Wendell Holmes' poem "Old Ironsides," published in the *Boston Daily Advertiser* in 1830. (The ship fought in the Tripolitan War and the War of 1812 and was rebuilt twice, in 1833 and in 1877. It is on exhibition today at the Boston Navy Yard.)

87 (c) The Viennese violinist (1875–1962) created a brilliant repertory of subtly baroque flavor, claiming that he had found the hitherto unknown manuscripts by Paganini, Tartini, Boccherini and others "in libraries and monasteries while visiting Rome, Florence, Venice and Paris." He revealed his deception in 1935.

193

88 (a) The Continental Army then moved north and camped near the Hudson River at New Windsor, New York. General George Washington set up headquarters at Newburgh, and he remained there until August 1783. The Treaty of Paris was signed on April 19, 1783—eight years from the date of the battle of Lexington, which was a year before the colonists even decided definitely on independence—but Washington, who had retreated from New York City in 1776, didn't ride triumphantly back into New York until December 4, 1783.

89 (b) And only one president remained a bachelor: James Buchanan (1791–1868). Grover Cleveland (1837–1908), who had, as a young bachelor in Buffalo, fathered a child, was a bachelor still when he was first elected president in 1884, but married his ward midway through his first term.

90 (a),(b),(c),(d) The muckraker (1878–1968) had lived for seven unforgettable weeks among the stockyard workers, and his tale was right from the horse's mouth. The odor of the men who shoveled fertilizer scared any ordinary visitor at one hundred yards.

91 (b) The Democratic party's strength lay in the South, which was profoundly Protestant and would not look with favor on having Mrs. Dewey's religion in the White House.

92 (c) "Neither slavery nor involuntary servitude, except as a punishment for crime whereof the party shall have been duly convicted, shall exist within the United States, or any place subject to their jurisdiction."

93 (a) The Mississippian was never brought to trial for treason, because of legal difficulties, and refused to enter government again—he easily could have secured a seat in the Senate again. He even refused to regain his citizenship or to request formal amnesty. When he died, in New Orleans, he was given a hero's funeral.

94 (b) Summaries were not published until 1821.

95 (c) The scion of President John Tyler's secretary of war and two crew members without political influence—a gunner's mate and a boatswain's mate—were hanged at sea, in 1842, after the *Somers* had carried to the African coast dispatches for Com-

modore Matthew C. Perry's squadron. Spencer confessed that
he had also entertained mutinous ideas while serving on two
other Navy ships. "A brazier of hot coals was brought and then
applied to the tube and priming of a long cannonade; on the
report, the drums rolled; the command was given, the crew
hauled lustily on the tails, and the three bodies, still manacled
and with their heads enwrapped in pea-jackets, swung from the
mainyard." In a rough sea and by lantern light, the three bodies
were committed to the deep. A naval historian has noted that
the affair—Spencer's influential father tried to wreck the career
of the *Somers'* commanding officer, Alexander Slidell Mack-
enzie—"had one important and far-reaching effect; it centered
public attention upon the demoralizing practice of forcing into
the Navy occasional unprincipled young rascals, without training, whose only qualification was political pull. In that way, it
helped to pave the way for the establishment of the Naval School,
from which the United States Naval Academy of today has
grown. The new Naval School raised a barrier against the in-
trusion of midshipmen who were unfitted for their duties; the
standards of admission have been steadily rising since."

96 (c) "The more I see of the czar, the kaiser, and the mikado,"
TR declared, "the better I am content with democracy."

97 (b) The black intellectuals had agreed that the time was ripe for
organized, determined and aggressive action that would lead to
immediate black freedom and growth in the United States.
America's ten million blacks, "stolen, ravished, degraded—
struggling up through difficulties and oppression—need sympathy but receive criticism, need help but are given hindrance,
need protection but are given mob violence, need justice but
are given charity, need leadership but are given cowardice and
apology, need bread but are given a stone." The meeting took
place on the Canadian side of the falls because no New York
manor would let in the delegates.

98 (c) Preaching his *Gospel of Beauty*—the things most worthwhile
are one's own heart and neighborhood—the poet (1879–1931)
walked in 1912 from his home in Springfield, Illinois, to New
Mexico, wearing yellow corduroys and an oriflamme tie and
carrying on his back an oilcloth packet of poems.

99 (d) Calhoun directed Southern interests, especially on slavery, for sixteen years. A year before his death—his last words were "The South, the poor South"—Calhoun predicted that the blacks and the profligate whites who might unite with them would become the principal recipients of federal offices and patronage and would, in consequence, be raised above the whites of the South in the political and social scale. Slavery, to the former "war hawk," presidential candidate, and secretary of war in the Monroe Administration, was "a positive good." (The only other veep to resign was compelled to do so: Spiro Agnew [1918–   ] was charged in 1973 with having taken kickbacks when he was governor of Maryland.)

100 (a) In 1910 Berger (1860–1929) became the first Socialist to sit in Congress, but he was barred later for antiwar views. He was readmitted to the House in 1923 and served three more terms.

101 (b) Threat of a new civil war hung over the House of Representatives in 1876 when its specially created electoral commission, voting along strict party lines, gave the Republican Hayes (1822–1893) the controversial nineteenth presidency by one vote, though it was thought by many, including most Democrats, that the Democratic candidate, Samuel Jones Tilden (1814–1886), the reform governor of New York, had really won the election of 1876. Fraud was committed by both parties in the South, still partly occupied by federal troops. An investigation into the "stolen election" was aborted, and, in turn, Reconstruction government came to an end in Dixie.

102 (d) "No other First Lady in history has had her influence, no other has been so much the center of controversy, and no other has so affected the lives of the women who followed her," the author Abigail Q. McCarthy declared before a gathering in late 1982 of authors, journalists and former White House aides, who agreed with the one hundred history professors that Mrs. Roosevelt (1884–1962) was the most distinguished of First Ladies.

103 (b) William Franklin (1731–1813), though condemned as a "virulent enemy of this country," was spared because of the reverence that the colonists had for his father. In 1780 George

III created an army under the direction of the Board of Associated Loyalists and it was headed by William Franklin.

104 (c) Lewis, who had been a private secretary to President Jefferson, was murdered in rural Tennessee in 1809. Clark became governor of the Missouri Territory (1813–1821), and died in 1838.

105 (b) The historian Thomas Flexner has written, "In all history no general had ever been more strangely and momentously commissioned. Far from stepping to the head of a constituted force, the commander in chief was the only man (no rifleman having yet been enlisted) actually to be enrolled in the Continental Army. Not by any direct vote or broad decision had Congress brought the thirteen colonies into the war being waged in New England, but by the act of elevating Washington. There was no nation to fight for: the Declaration of Independence lay more than a year in the future. There was, except for intangibles—grievances and resented atrocities—only Washington."

106 (d) The vivacious Jennie Jerome (1854–1921), a New Yorker and one-sixteenth Iroquois, married Lord Randolph Churchill in 1874; two years later she prematurely delivered Winston in a ladies' cloakroom in the Churchill ancestral castle of Blenheim, where she was attending a dance. Jennie was named for Jenny Lind, the Swedish Nightingale, with whom her father had had a relationship. (Lord Randolph died in 1894 of syphilis, raving mad.)

107 (c) The Supreme Court in 1915 had ruled that movies were not protected by the First Amendment, so communities across the country—with their new freedom—declared motion pictures off-limits if they made crime look glamorous or presented a viewpoint that violated moral and religious taboos. (Because the adulterous Hedy Lamarr's facial expressions during orgasm were found to be obscene and the theme of the film immoral, a print of *Ecstasy* was burned by a federal marshal in 1935. In 1952 the Court reversed itself and held that films were indeed worthy of First Amendment protection.)

108 (d) The First Lady of Contraception, a trained maternity nurse, was sentenced to a month in a workhouse for founding a birth-control clinic in the Brownsville section of Brooklyn, New

York, in 1916. (Brownsville was largely a Jewish neighbor-hood, and some of its residents suspected that the general purpose of Mrs. Sanger's campaign was genocide against Jews.) She also was arrested for sending birth-control information through the mail. She vowed that the curse of Eve must be lifted. (*Birth Control*, a film about Mrs. Sanger's activities, was banned in 1917 by New York authorities, who called it "immoral, indecent, and directly contrary to public welfare.")

109 (d) There already was a Society for the Prevention of Cruelty to Animals. (Even after the turn of the century, pre-teen children were working in chemical plants at two in the morning.)

110 (c) Washington himself presided at the trial, which convicted Dr. Church (1734–1778) of "criminal correspondence with the enemy; he had revealed Minutemen arms data to the British in Boston. The Son of Liberty was imprisoned and deported, and he drowned when the ship carrying him to the West Indies sank in a storm.

111 (b) At the time, 1796, presidential electors were chosen in ac-cordance with local state law, and each elector then cast his ballot for two presidential candidates. The candidate with the most votes became president, the candidate with the second most votes became the vice president. The *Federalist* candi-date, John Adams, received seventy-one votes, and the *Re-publican* candidate, Thomas Jefferson, was the runner-up, with sixty-eight, nine more votes than Adams' running mate, Charles Pinckney. Jefferson had run with Aaron Burr, who received only thirty votes. In 1800, Jefferson and running mate Burr unexpectedly tied for the presidency, at seventy-three votes each (President Adams was third in his re-election bid), and the decision for the first and only time was left to the House of Representatives. The more popular author of the Declaration of Independence and apostle of agrarian democracy was elected after a long deadlock, largely because the influential Alexander Hamilton had advised the Federalists to support Jefferson as less dangerous than Burr. (Burr, deflected in his later bid for the governorship of New York State, again by Hamilton's influence, was to kill Hamilton in a duel.)

112 (d) Edward Bellamy's futuristic Utopian novel, published in 1888, commended the most revolutionary changes imaginable—a society without lawyers, bankers, stockbrokers and merchants. There would be no longer rich or poor. Every human being counted alike in the capacity to earn and the right to receive a competency. The wealth-producing power of the community was enormously increased by elimination of waste and by the application of simple principles that elicited the best work from every citizen. Money was no longer used. Credit and debt disappeared. All the uncertainties of fortunes that impel men to struggle and contend for wealth were eliminated. Education was universal. Ignorance, crime, vice were unknown in this brave new world. To stabilize international relations, Bellamy predicted a world federal union of national syndicates; world trade would be balanced with national surpluses. *Looking Backward* helped to create a consciousness and a climate for "economic democratization," which culminated decades later in projects like the New Deal—but not in the "classless society" that Bellamy (1850–1898) claimed to desire.

113 (c) Franklin Roosevelt will thus be the only president to be elected to a third and then to a fourth term.

114 (d) The *Times* apologized in 1969 to Goddard's widow a few days before Neil Armstrong became the first man to step on the planet's only satellite. (The *Times*, just before the Wrights successfully flew a motorized aeroplane, editorialized, "Time and money spent in airship experiments are wasted.")

115 (b) The price of tea had been reduced recently.

116 (a) *Dred, A Tale of the Great Dismal Swamp*, was not in the same league with *Uncle Tom's Cabin*, but "the little lady who made the great war" (in Abraham Lincoln's words) was able again to itemize the moral evils of slavery, though this time the base was economics: free markets, such as there were in the North, were so much better for the businessman than was slavery. The setting was the Utopian life on a Canadian farm. An abolitionist guides his slaves toward gradual freedom.

117 (c) Canada.

199

118 (d) The plan for four time zones was officially recognized in 1883, and it did much to relieve chaos among the railways.

119 (b) During Thomas Jefferson's Administration (1801–1809), it would have taken $3 million to buy our "Antilles heel," but the nation didn't have it. By 1861, only three countries in the western world still condoned slavery: Cuba, Brazil and the United States.

120 (a) Charles Curtis (1860–1936) was the descendant of a Kaw. Before 1929 he had been both a Congressman and a senator (Kansas). In 1924 he was the majority leader in the Senate.

121 (a) Allied and British commissioners discussed the terms of surrender in the ground floor to the left of the chimney at the rear of the Surrender House.

122 (d) Lt. Col. George Armstrong Custer (1839–1876) and his troops (225 men) were massacred by Sitting Bull and the Sioux at Little Big Horn in the Dakota territory in 1876, three months before the United States celebrated its centennial. In the Civil War, Custer had earned a reputation for daring and brilliance in battle.

123 (b) The poet and public official and erstwhile lawyer (1892–1982) served as librarian of Congress, assistant director of the Office of War Information and a Harvard professor. His poetry and verse drama won Pulitzer Prizes.

124 (d) Clinton (1769–1828), once New York's most powerful politico, was governor when "Clinton's ditch"—the Erie Canal— was opened in 1825. As a United States senator, he introduced the Twelfth Amendment—state electors would cast ballots and thereby select the president and the vice-president. (When James A. Garfield was elected president in 1880, he was also elected an Ohio senator; at the time he was an Ohio congressman.)

125 (b) The poet was Margaret Mead (1901–1978), and the publication was the *New Republic* in 1932. Her national reputation had been established four years earlier with the publication of her best selling, and later controversial, work of anthropology, *Coming of Age in Samoa.*

126 (d) The polio-stricken governor of New York State flew in a flimsy trimotor airplane from Albany to Chicago in 1932.

127 (a) The yo-yo, discovered in the Philippines by Mr. Duncan, was originally a Far Eastern jungle weapon that could be bounced off the head of an enemy and swiftly drawn up out of sight by someone hidden in a tree.

128 (c) The effect of power on presidents, Mr. Adams (1838–1918) wrote, "has been always tragic, chiefly as an almost insane excitement at first and a worse reaction afterwards; but also because no mind is so well balanced as to bear the strain of seizing unlimited force without habit or knowledge of it; and finding it disputed with him by hungry packs of wolves and hounds whose lives depend on snatching the carrion. President [Theodore] Roosevelt [for instance] enjoys a singularly direct nature and honest intent, but he lives naturally in restless agitation that would have worn out most tempers in a month, and his first year of Presidency showed chronic excitement that made a friend tremble. Politics, as a practice, whatever its professions, has always been the systematic organization of hatred."

129 (d) The president and the nominee rode out the storm that erupted—Black had shared the views of most whites in his community—and the justice went on to become a constitutional libertarian, steadfastly and at times eloquently supporting individual liberties. Invariably his decisions transcended race, creed and religion. He played a critical and decisive part in the Warren Court's equal-rights decisions. He also helped to enlarge the rights of criminal suspects. (When the Klan reached the peak of its strength, in 1925, membership throughout the nation—but chiefly in the Southwest, Farm West and Middle West—numbered about five million.)

130 (d) The Little Giant (1813–1861) told the Great Emancipator before the inauguration, "In our devotion and attachment to the Constitution we have never differed—in this we are one—this must and shall not be destroyed," and he held the president's hat during Abraham Lincoln's inauguration speech in Washington. A loyal statesman, and one of the great orators of the day, he had a broad national vision. When he was fatally

201

stricken with typhoid fever in Springfield, Illinois, he was hailed by many as the "foremost patriot and statesman of his time."

131 (d) At the age of thirty-three, the crime investigator (1902–1971) had prosecuted mobsters like Louis "Lepke" Buchalter, Dutch Schultz and Lucky Luciano, who ran New York's gambling, loansharking and prostitution rackets. Dewey was elected governor of New York thrice, in 1942, 1946 and 1950.

132 (a) It was imposed to help finance the Civil War, and was for 3 percent on incomes over $800. The tax was later repealed. In 1913 the Sixteenth Amendment to the Constitution was ratified: "The Congress shall have power to lay and collect taxes on incomes, from whatever source derived." There is no chance that the amendment will be repealed.

133 (a) Helper became monomaniacal on the building of a railroad from Hudson's Bay to Patagonia and eventually killed himself.

134 (b) On his return from France in 1785, he served three annual terms as president of the Pennsylvania executive council, and his was an important voice in the Federal Constitutional Convention. Using opium to ease the unbearable pain of bladder stone and gout, he found himself addicted to the drug, explaining to James Madison that the best terms he could make with his complaint was to give up a part of his remaining life for the greater ease of the rest.

135 (d) The controversial and beloved Little Flower (1882–1947) was mayor of New York City for twelve years and then director general of the United Nation's Relief and Rehabilitation Agency.

136 (c) Dr. W. C. Minor, a surgeon-captain in the army of the North during the Civil War, suffered a mental breakdown when ordered to brand a soldier who had deserted. In England, where he had sought sanctuary, Dr. Minor committed a street killing brought on by a persecution mania. He was incarcerated for life in an asylum, from where he made his noteworthy contribution to lexicography.

137 (c) Stonewall Jackson was killed in the Civil War—probably shot by his own men—and Barbara Fritchie died before the authenticity of John Greenleaf Whittier's ballad could be verified, so we'll never know if she indeed faced down the Confederate army marching through Frederick, Maryland, that day in 1862. Southerners also liked the story, for Jackson, in a typically chivalrous gesture, cried out, "Who touches a hair of yon gray head, dies like a dog! March on!"

138 (d) The road test was delayed by an hour as workmen used the back of an axe to knock bricks out of the framework of the workshed so that the automobile could make its egress into the world. In 1908 Ford himself drove his all-black car from New York to Seattle in twenty-two days and fifty-five minutes. The first automobile trip across the United States from San Francisco to New York, in 1903, had taken fifty-two days. (The first coast-to-coast airplane flight, from New York to Pasadena, California, in 1911 took forty-nine days. The pilot was Galbraith P. Rodgers, and there were many, many layovers.)

139 (b) The two-minute speech was, of course, President Abraham Lincoln's Gettysburg Address. Everett immediately recognized its eloquence and raced across the platform to congratulate Mr. Lincoln. The next day he wrote the White House, "I should be glad if I could flatter myself that I came as near the central idea of the occasion in two hours as you did in two minutes." (Press disdain greeted Mr. Lincoln's speech. The Chicago *Times*, for one, felt that Americans should be embarrassed by the president's "dish-watery utterances.")

140 (c) Austin founded the first Anglo-American community in Texas in 1822. When Mexico abolished slavery, he supported a contract-labor law allowing slaves to be brought into Texas, technically as indentured servants. His mottoes were the redemption of Texas from the wilderness, fidelity and gratitude to his adopted country, and to be inflexibly true to the interests and just rights of his settlers.

141 (c) Abigail Adams (1744–1818), the testy unschooled daughter of a minister, did not live to see her son John Quincy become president in 1824, but her violent-tempered husband did; the short, plump Atlas of Independence was the longest-lived chief executive, dying at nearly ninety-one years at his home, Peacefield, in Quincy, Massachusetts, in the second year of his son's presidential term and on the fiftieth anniversary of the Declaration of Independence. (John and Abigail Adams were married for fifty-four years.)

142 (a) The "Sam Adams of Virginia" (1736–1799) was an outspoken early critic of England—"I know not what course others may take, but as for me, give me liberty or give me death!" He was a governor of Virginia and a member of the Continental Congress. After retiring from active public life, he developed a severe ailment of the intestine—intussusception—and his doctor became desperate when no cure could be found: the patient could take a dose of liquid mercury that, the doctor explained, could kill him or give him relief. The fearless Henry took his chances, drank the mercury and died.

143 (c) New Mexico finally won statehood in 1912, the same year as did Arizona.

144 (b) To escape the deep depression caused by the death of his wife, Bryant, an antislavery pro-Union editor and erstwhile lawyer, translated all of Homer into blank verse.

145 (d) Vermont was not to be a state, "the philosopher" (1738–1789) wrote, but a separate nation. When Allen subsequently was captured during a raid against Canada, he schemed with the British to make Vermont a British province or to aid Vermont to obtain separate status.

146 (a) The horticulturalist (1849–1926) was charged with blasphemy and denounced by churches for "interfering with nature" and bringing forth new creations. Many of his specimens have bloomed.

147 (c) Until there was a pay raise in 1814, congressmen were paid six dollars per diem when Congress was in session.

148 (d) And he did, in 1910. "It will be the greatest disappointment of my life," Clemens, or Mark Twain, had written, "if I don't go out with Halley's comet."

149 (c) The case went all the way up to the Supreme Court, which turned down the plaintiff in 1876.

150 (d) Hattie W. Caraway (1878–1950) was first chosen in a special election in 1931 to complete the term of her late husband, Thaddeus H. Caraway, of Arkansas. (The first woman to serve in the Senate was suffragette Rebecca Latimer Felton. She was eighty-seven years old and served for only one day, November 21, 1922; her appointment was a token gesture by the governor of Georgia, who had opposed the suffrage amendment which became law earlier in the year.) Mrs. Caraway, in 1943, was cosponsor of an equal-rights amendment.

151 (d) Until then the tomato had been merely an exotic curiosity, used as an ornamental shrub and considered poisonous. Johnson did not fall frothing to the ground—and from that day to this, the safe old reliable tomato has been a favorite vegetable.

152 (b) Steel girders, rather than the walls, could indeed carry the weight of the building, and the skyscraper, incorporating the new concepts of steel frame and elevator that liberated design, was the perfect architectural expression of American optimism and faith in progress—up, up and away.

153 (c) Many years later, Frank Sinatra, alluding to technical advances, said, "If it hadn't been for the genius of RCA chairman David Sarnoff, no one would have ever heard of me."

154 (c) *Little Women* was largely her autobiographical story of New England family life. *Little Men* was based on the experiences of her nephews.

155 (a) Nearly one hundred fifty years after the American Revolution.

156 (d) When the union among the original thirteen states became an actuality in 1781, the title President of the United States in Congress Assembled was bestowed upon John Hanson, who was representing Maryland. Most of the first session of the Senate, from April 23 to May 14, 1789, was consumed with debate over what to call the nation's chief executive.

157 (a) Hamilton

158 (c) Elbert Hubbard (1856–1915), the long-haired editor of the *Philistine*, sold one hundred million copies of *his* four-page exhortation.

159 (a) The general in chief, a former superintendent of West Point, had already turned down command of the Union army and retired to his home (now the white-pillared mansion in Arlington Cemetery).

160 (b) Tudor (1783–1864) figured out how to "harvest" and keep ice from melting and to ship it successfully to the warmest ports, from Martinique to India. Hailed as a miracle-worker, the flamboyant, defiant, energetic, reckless, imperious, vain, contemptuous Tudor had as his creed: "He who gives back at the first repulse and without striking the second blow despairs of success, has never been, is not and never will be a hero in war, love or business." At the age of fifty, he married a nineteen-year-old girl and fathered six children.

161 (c) Guiteau, after a long, stormy trial, was judged sane and guilty and then hanged in 1882, nearly a year after President James Garfield died from the gunshot wound. Guiteau had been a disgruntled office-seeker, and the assassination prompted Congress to legislate the Civil Service Commission, replacing the spoils system with a merit system.

162 (c) Under a flag of truce, Francis Scott Key (1779–1843) was seeking the release of a captured friend from the British fleet bombarding Baltimore in 1814. He was detained overnight on an enemy vessel, so that he would not reveal information about the British that he might have obtained. By the dawn's early light, he was so pleased to see the American flag (thirty feet by forty-two feet) still waving proudly over Fort McHenry in the harbor that he scribbled a poem, "The Defence of Fort McHenry," that could be sung to the popular English drinking song, "Anacreon in Heaven," composed by John Stafford Smith for the Anacreontic Society of London. Key's title was changed about a month after the poem was first published. More than a century later, President Hoover signed the act making Key's poem the national anthem. (Key was a devout lay reader in the Episcopal Church and wrote many songs on religious themes.)

163 (d) Leon Edel, the literary critic and biographer, has noted that at one end of town Ralph Waldo Emerson was faithfully recording his daily aphorisms, and Nathaniel Hawthorne was setting down his American notebooks at the other. In between, the Alcotts, father and daughter, Bronson and Louisa, confided daily thoughts and happenings to paper, as did sundry other transcendentalists—Channings and Sanburns and various other worthies—"all seeking to seize the moment, to arrest time in its flight." And, of course, there was Henry David Thoreau, scratching his steel pen nib across wide sheets of paper in the Texas Street house that he had helped his father to build.

164 (c) In the second third of the sixteenth century, the Spanish explorer (1510–1554) roamed from Mexico to the Gulf of California, Arizona, New Mexico, Texas, northern Kansas to the Nebraska border, south to the Rio Grande, westward through the Zuñi country and Cíbola, through mountain passes again and down the Gulf of California to Mexico City.

165 (d) The self-promoting Connecticut Yankee served two terms in the state legislature (1865–1869) and two years as mayor. He was an unsuccessful candidate for Congress in 1867.

166 (a) The president, who was born on the ninety-sixth anniversary of the Declaration of Independence, slept an average of eleven hours in every twenty-four. He could pronounce the word *cow* in four syllables, thanks in part to his nasal twang. He was the first president to have the oath of office administered by a former president—the chief justice was William Howard Taft, the twenty-sixth president. (Mr. Taft also administered the oath to Herbert Hoover in 1929.)

167 (c) By the time that Edison was able to produce (in 1909) an improved, rechargeable battery that really worked, the internal combustion engine was the king of the road. But Edison's unit became the workhorse in mining, on shipboard and for telegraphy, submarines and railway signaling.

168 (c) The Bill of Rights was an indictment of the rule of James II, whose violation of constitutional rights (the Bill said) freed Englishmen from their allegiance.

169 (b) His original nickname was Nigger Jack. (His American Expeditionary Force arrived in Europe two months after the United

207

States had entered the First World War, but it didn't clash in force with the Huns for a year after that.)

170 (d) He was a founder and the first president of the National Academy of Design and for forty years professor of painting and sculpture at the University of the City of New York. In his old age the nativist hated Abraham Lincoln, agreeing with those who thought slavery "divinely ordained."

171 (b) Eight were born in Virginia and seven in Ohio.

172 (d) Four years after her husband, Franklin, had died during his unprecedented fourth term as president, Mrs. Roosevelt (1884– 1962) publicly confessed that she had never wanted her husband to be in the White House. "It was pure selfishness on my part," she wrote, "and I never mentioned my feelings on the subject to him." (Nancy Reagan also has admitted that she did not want her husband to run for the presidency.)

173 (b) Morris (1734–1806) had been financially ruined in land speculation; he was confined for several years in Philadelphia. He had signed the Declaration of Independence though he had voted against its adoption.

174 (c) A tiny, indomitable woman, Miss Royall (1769–1854) was a consummate individualist, crusading against governmental evils, exposing graft and incompetence. Her newspapers, *Paul Pry* and later the *Huntress*, were hand-to-mouth operations printed on battered little presses from type discarded by other papers.

175 (a) Her former lover—a voluptuary, and the nation's most prominent architect—was shot by her (literally) insanely jealous husband, Harry Thaw, at the roof theater of Madison Square Garden in 1906. "The most sensational trial of its time revealed to plain people everywhere the hypocrisy of Victorian morality." The exquisite twenty-two-year-old former artist's model and show girl—"the girl in the red velvet swing"—was described as a "tigress between two men, egging them on." Thaw spent much of fifteen years in asylums, then in semiseclusion until his death in 1947. Evelyn told her "own true story" to all comers. She died at the age of eighty-two in 1967 in a convalescent home, "knowing only too well that her lovely young self had died that night sixty years earlier at the roof garden."

176 (d) The Irish-born Herbert in 1940, the Russian-born Stravinsky in 1982. They were both naturalized citizens.

177 (a) Brought to heel by the president, Secretary William Seward (1801–1872) then performed the functions of his office with great skill, and was a dominant force in the cabinet. Assassins also tried to kill him when they murdered the president in 1865; he somewhat regained his health after having been stabbed and in 1867 negotiated the purchase of "Seward's Folly"— Alaska—from Russia, planning (before he had to leave office with President Andrew Johnson) to annex Hawaii and Santo Domingo.

178 (c) The Indian was the Cherokee genius Sequoyah (c. 1770–1843), who had made the tribe literate. He was president of the Western Cherokee, serving as arbiter between his group and the Eastern Cherokee, who were forcibly moved to the Indian territory now Oklahoma by United States troops. When a question was put to him, Sequoyah would, according to custom, ponder for a considerable time before replying, often taking a whiff of his calumet while reflecting on the answers.

179 (d) Richard Stockton, a graduate of the university that became Princeton, had been a successful lawyer. He chose to remain in Congress instead of taking the post of chief justice of New Jersey. When the British overran the state, he was betrayed and captured. Imprisonment broke his health, and he was an invalid until he died in 1781.

180 (a) On Sunday, April 14, 1861, after Major Robert Anderson had saluted his flag with fifty guns, the garrison was conveyed to the fleet in Charleston harbor. Despite their defeat, the men were greeted with enthusiasm at New York when they arrived on the nineteenth. Passenger steamers welcomed them with echoing whistles, cheer after cheer went up from craft in the harbor, and distinguished visitors boarded the soldiers' steamer to give a hearty greeting. For weeks afterward, when a member of the garrison was recognized in the streets, it became the signal for an ovation.

181 (c) Forty years later the courageous abolitionist, editor and former slave (1817–1895) was to say, "There are few facts in my humble history to which I look back with more satisfaction than to the fact, recorded in the history of the woman suffrage movement, that I was sufficiently enlightened at the early day, when only a few years from slavery, to support your resolution for woman suffrage. I have done very little in this world in which to glory, except this one act—and I certainly glory in that. When I ran away from slavery, it was for myself; when I advocated emancipation, it was for my people; but when I stood up for the rights of woman, self was out of the question, and I found a little nobility in the act." Yet, he was to be criticized by some women's rightists for accepting the vote for blacks before women, black or white. He became marshal of the District of Columbia (1877–1881) and U.S. minister to Haiti (1889–1891).

182 (d) The congressional act was signed into law by President Dwight D. Eisenhower, and the first checks ($25,000 each) went out two and a half months later to Herbert Hoover and Harry S. Truman. The bill also authorized $50,000 annually for office help, unlimited free mailings and free office space.

183 (c) Davis (1808–1889), who was to become president of the Confederacy, was an ardent expansionist. Requesting congressional funds, he wrote, "...Napoleon when in Egypt used with marked success the dromedary... in subduing the Arabs, whose habits and country were very similar to those of the mounted Indians of our Western plains... For like military purposes, for expresses, and for reconnaissances, it is believed, the dromedary would supply a want now seriously felt in our services; and for transportation with troops rapidly moving across the country, the camel, it is believed, would remove an obstacle which now serves greatly to diminish the value and efficiency of our troops on the Western frontier..." Thirty-four camels from Tunis, Malta, Smyrna, Salonica and Constantinople were shipped into San Antonio. Texans walked miles simply to gawk at the aliens, which proved partial to mesquite, cactus, greasewood and creosote bush. The camels stalked to Fort Defiance, New Mexico, and along the Colorado River and to California and back to Texas. They could be more easily worked than mules. Forty-four more camels were brought in from the Middle East by the government and fifteen were imported from China by a private company. After government interest in the camels ceased, the beasts of burden were used by business to haul freight and ore, for survey trips, road construction, circuses and zoos, carrying salt and as racing animals—a camel can outrun a quarter horse in a short race. They became a road hazard (the smell of a camel makes horses panic in revulsion) and laws against unattended camels were enacted. (In 1861, President Abraham Lincoln politely refused an offer of dozens of elephants from the King of Siam.)

184 (d) Sen. Alan Cranston, after returning in the late 1930s from Europe, where he had served as a correspondent for International News Service, published an abridged translation of *Mein Kampf*. Germany's all-time bestselling author—and dictator—was able to halt the book's distribution on the ground of copyright infringement. (Sales of the book made the Führer a millionaire. Of course, few German households felt secure without a copy in full view.)

185 (b) The Escadrille, formed in April 1916, was a French pursuit squadron manned by one-hundred and eighty Americans while the United States was still neutral in the First World War. Prince (1887–1916) died two days after a freak landing accident; he was awarded the Legion of Honor on his deathbed. In 1918, the Escadrille became part of the American Air Service under General William Mitchell.

186 (c) The District of Columbia.

187 (c) He was imprisoned in Florida and in Alabama and then became a farmer and a member of the Dutch Reformed Church on a military reservation in Oklahoma. For gambling, he was expelled by the church. When he died he had become a wizened curiosity on the reservation.

188 (c) It could be used to sneak up on and place explosive charges against the hulls of enemy vessels. France—Napoleon!—and England encouraged its development; the United States did not. Fulton's *North River Steam Boat*, based in the Hudson River at Clermont, New York, was the first financially successful steamboat after John Fitch's original steamboat, plying the Delaware River between Philadelphia and Trenton, had fallen on hard times.

189 (d) The hatchet-swinging reformer (1846–1911), once married to an alcoholic, spent her life protesting "evils" of tobacco, foreign food, corsets and booze. She was arrested at least thirty times and died at the edge of madness. Her mother *was* mad and a rebel: she believed she was Queen Victoria and would wear royal purple robes and ride around in a carriage upholstered with plush. Her horses had silver-mounted harnesses, and a tall Negro in a scarlet hunting jacket would precede her—blowing a trumpet to herald the queen's arrival, of course.)

190 (d) The commander (1860–1948) of the American Expeditionary Force in France in the First World War was nominated by Congress to the post after the Armistice.

191 (d) Frances Perkins (1882–1965) was industrial commissioner for New York State under Governor Franklin Roosevelt before he as president appointed her to be secretary of labor. She served for twelve years.

192 (b) He built his Wall Street reputation by organizing Republic Steel, helping to finance Kaiser-Frazer's automobile business, and taking a majority position in the Chesapeake and Ohio Railroad. After meeting Nikita Khrushchev in Moscow, Eaton (1883–1979) undertook speaking tours to persuade the public that the nuclear arms race should be abandoned.

193 (b) They had plotted their trip after the uprising of 1830 had put on the throne the "Citizen King," Louis Philippe. As were many other young Republicans, the pair were out of sympathy with the new regime and politically in a dangerous position. As a way to escape Restoration, they convinced the government that they should make a firsthand study of American prison systems. They sailed, looking to America as a sanctuary of liberty and equality. They returned still convinced of the value of the American system of democratic government, though both had many criticisms, and they wrote their report on the American penitentiary system and proposals for its application in France. Their study was favorably received, and other European governments sent prison-survey missions to the United States. France built some prisons on the general principles of the Pennsylvania system of solitary confinement but soon adopted exile as the program for dealing with criminals, a solution that Tocqueville and Beaumont had opposed.

194 (d) The astronomer, working at the Lowell Observatory in Arizona in 1930, discovered the outermost planet so far seen in our solar system when he looked on a series of film plates containing hundreds of thousands of stars. He had been looking for the gravitational force that perturbs the giant planets Uranus and Neptune. (Pluto is too small to cause their irregular orbits; the combined mass of Pluto and its lone moon, Charon (discovered in 1978 in synchronous orbit 12,000 miles above the surface of the planet), is only one-fifth that of earth's moon.) The search for Planet X continues.

195 (a) Andrew Mellon (1855–1937) was seventy-four years old— and fabulously wealthy. Twelve million people would be out of work and uncounted savings lost during the long Depression.

196 (d) Flashed from Promontory, Utah, on May 10, 1869.

197 (a) Cleveland (1837–1908), who was the state's governor, became the twenty-second president by a margin of thirty-seven electoral votes nationally.

198 (c) Monroe (1758–1831), the fifth president, was unopposed in 1820 when there was not yet a party system. The single dissenting ballot was cast by John Quincy Adams (231–1), who did so in order that the father of our country would always be the lone unanimously elected chief executive. (Until 1824 presidential candidates were chosen by party caucus and then selected by the electoral college—the citizenry did not vote.)

199 (b) If the Bostonians were captured, they would be hanged.

200 (d) "A short stout-built man, stooping as he walked, speaking in a high key, addicted to snuff, and with a keen gray eye that lighted up a plain face with shrewd expression," the diligent editor-publisher (the Stone analogy) was an earnest advocate of the Union, internal improvements and protection to industry. It has been said that he was as influential as any in the nationalist economic school that sponsored the American system after the War of 1812: "Britain has destroyed more men in

213

Asia than all France possessed, but the King is gentle, magnanimous and just . . ."

201 (c) To the chief executive, to be or not to be continued to be *the* question. "The forest and water problems," TR had declared in a "big stick" message to Congress, "are perhaps the most vital internal problems of the United States," and he demanded that Congress protect hundreds of millions of acres as forest and mineral preserves. As a "warm believer in reclamation and forestry," he was willing to go out on the limb. (By the 1890s the Department of the Interior was characterized by collusion with lumber-industry interests, turning the landscape into a wasteland.) Pinchot went on to become governor of Pennsylvania, running in the progressive spirit against the old guard of the Republican party, eliminating a $30 million deficit and revising laws providing for the care of the insane.

202 (d) A white man, Shaw (1837–63) was born in Boston to wealth and gentility, and was committed to the antislavery crusade. He died leading a charge of the 54th Massachusetts Regiment against the gates of Charleston. Shaw's sacrifice inspired Emerson to write, "So nigh is grandeur to our dust, So near is God to man, When duty whispers low, *Thou must*, The youth replies, I can." (Approximately eighteen thousand blacks served in the Union army—about 10 percent of the total force—and seventeen were awarded the Congressional Medal of Honor.)

203 (a) The first to open was the Franklin D. Roosevelt Library at Hyde Park, and the most recent to open was the Gerald R. Ford Library in Ann Arbor, Michigan. The other five are the Herbert Hoover Library, West Branch, Iowa; the Lyndon B. Johnson Library, Austin, Texas; the Dwight D. Eisenhower Library, Abilene, Kansas; the Harry S. Truman Library, Independence, Missouri, and the John. F. Kennedy Library, Boston, Massachusetts.

204 (d) The genius (1879–1955), a naturalized American, would have been the first president of Israel, but he said, "I have neither the natural ability nor the experience necessary to deal with human beings and to carry out official functions."

214

205 (b) Mr. Nixon (1913–   ) lost in 1960 to John F. Kennedy, but came back in 1968 to defeat Hubert Humphrey. When he was reelected in 1972, defeating George McGovern, Mr. Nixon won the electoral vote of forty-eight states—*the* landslide in presidential elections. (1972 was, of course, the year of the Watergate "tricks.")

206 (a) Washington wanted California before the British or the French laid hands on it, but Mexico would not negotiate its sale. General Winfield Scott's siege of the powerful fortress of Vera Cruz, in March 1847, was the first large-scale (ten thousand troops) amphibious operation in United States military history. On September 14, Scott entered Mexico City and a battalion of Marines began guard of the "halls of Montezuma." In the Treaty of Guadalupe-Hidalgo, in early 1848, Mexico ceded Texas to the Rio Grande, New Mexico and upper California in return for $15 million; that territory now includes California, Arizona, Nevada, Utah, parts of New Mexico, Colorado and Wyoming.

207 (b) The speech took the Democratic Convention by storm and he won the nomination. In all he lost three runs for the presidency, and died in Dayton, Tennessee, shortly after explaining on the witness stand his fundamentalist views on creation in the historic Scopes trial.

208 (c) "Ararat" would be a forty-eight-square-mile, white-oak forested city of refuge between Buffalo and Niagara Falls, New York. A dedication ceremony was held in 1825, but Noah soon left the area and the dream evaporated.

209 (d) It was repealed by the Twenty-first Amendment in 1933.

210 (a) Associate Justice Wilson (1742–1798), who had been instrumental in establishing the Constitution, was appointed by President George Washington and took the judicial oath on October 5, 1789. Scottish born, Wilson was described as one of the deepest thinkers and most exact reasoners in the Federal Convention of 1787.

211 (b) In June 1844 a dissenting Mormon group published an attack on Smith, and on June 27 he and his brother were dragged from a jail in Carthage, Illinois, by a mob of anti-Mormons and shot. A full-scale local war broke out against the Mormons. Smith became a martyr, and his memory healed the church breach. Under the leadership of Brigham Young, "the Lion of the Lord," the Mormons headed west from Nauvoo (Commerce, Illinois), across Iowa, along the north side of the Platte River, over part of the Oregon Trail, through South Pass in the Rockies to Fort Bridger in Wyoming and on to the "Great Basin" (Salt Lake Valley).

212 (a) In the decade before the Civil War, the future president (1822–1885) resigned his army commission under the pressure of allegations of intemperate drinking. He was a clerk in the family leather shop in Galena, Illinois, at the outbreak of the war, and he ended up the commanding field general for the Union.

213 (b) The letter made no mention of the silence, but it ignited a voluminous correspondence between Monticello, Virginia, and Quincy, Massachusetts, on the problems and future of the nation. The two died on the very same day, the Fourth of July, 1826, the fiftieth anniversary of the Declaration of Independence. Adams' last words were "Jefferson still lives," but Jefferson had died a few hours earlier. Celebration of the Fourth, which included fireworks for the first time, was not dampened; word of Jefferson's demise did not reach Washington until July 6, and news of Adams' death did not reach the capital for another two days. Our fifth president, James Monroe, also died on a Fourth of July, in 1831. (Calvin Coolidge is the only president to have been born on the Fourth, of 1872.)

214 (a) Up to that time, and even for a period afterward, mail was paid for by the recipient.

215 (d) Cosmic rays.

216 (b) A year after signing the Declaration of Independence, the forty-four-year-old chief executive of Georgia, and commander in chief of its army, was killed in a duel. Collectors have paid as much as sixteen thousand dollars for his signature.

217 (d) He was its president for one year. (Mr. Gulick had devised, in collaboration with one of his students, James Naismith, the game of basketball, at Springfield (Massachusetts) College, and he originated the triangle as the emblem of the YMCA, denoting the physical, social and spiritual aims of the Y.)

218 (a) Ulysses S. Grant's and John F. Kennedy's. President Kennedy, who was assassinated in 1963 at the age of forty-six, was the lone president to be survived by both parents.

219 (c) Paine (1737–1809) was prosecuted for attacks on English institutions (*The Rights of Man*) and fled (1792) to Paris, where he became a citizen and a member of the Convention and was imprisoned (1793) for anti-Jacobinism (*The Age of Reason*). He was rescued by his old friend James Monroe; the future president declared that Paine was an American citizen, and he then helped to nurse him back to health. Paine was ostracized on his return to the United States for a venomous letter he had sent to George Washington, for rumored adulterousness and for acknowledged drunkardness. On his death Paine's stateless remains were sent by a patron, the reformer William Cobbett, to England, where they passed into the hands of a furniture dealer and vanished forever. At the time of his death, Paine was believed to have accomplished more for human freedom, for the abolition of physical and mental slavery and for the brotherhood of mankind than any other American then living.

220 (a) There would be outright federal grants of two hundred dollars a month to everyone over sixty years of age, providing he "shall not engage in any gainful pursuit."

221 (c) Da Gama sailed up the east coast of Africa as far as Malindi (in modern Kenya), where an Arab pilot led the ships through the "ocean gates" across the Indian Ocean and to the Far East. If Bartholomew Diaz's voyage had been successful around the Cape of Good Hope in 1488, Columbus might never have sailed across the Atlantic—for whatever reason.

222 (b) The Reverend Edward Everett Hale (1822–1909) wrote the story "The Brick Moon" for the *Atlantic Monthly* (1870). Mr. Hale, who also wrote the classic short story "The Man Without a Country," suggested that brick might have been able to travel safely through the heat of atmospheric friction.

223 (c) Dahl's sentence was reduced to life imprisonment, then in 1940 he was given his freedom. ("Mrs. Dahl," the leader of an all-

girl dance combo, had merely pretended to be married to her
lover.)

224 (a) "If I had been technically trained," Mr. Gillette said, "I would
have quit."

225 (d) Haywood (1869–1928) was the radical one-eyed founder of
the Industrial Workers of the World (the Wobblies). He fled
the United States after a 138-day sedition trial, and for the
most part was ignored in Russia by the new Soviet leaders.
Reed (1887–1920), a Harvard graduate, headed the Communist Labor party in the United States and became a friend
of Lenin. He wrote *Ten Days That Shook the World*, an eye-
witness account of the Russian revolution, and was imprisoned
for smuggling diamonds.

226 (c) "Our party stands uncovered at the bier of Warren G. Harding"
was changed to "... at the grave of Warren G. Harding" so
that "dry" delegates would not be offended.

227 (c) About thirty-five armed blacks, including the fifty-five-year-
old preacher-carpenter Vesey, were captured and hanged in
1822. A house slave apparently tipped off authorities to the
Vesey plot.

228 (b) The conspirators included the governor of New York and the
mayor of New York City, both Tories, and Washington's body-
guard, Thomas Hickey. Hickey was court-martialed and hanged
for mutiny, sedition and treachery.

229 (c) Mrs. Dodge (1831–1905) turned to writing when her husband
died. *Hans Brinker*, published in 1865, was a carefully researched story.

230 (c) A graduate of the Naval Academy in 1846, Rear Admiral Carter
served as commandant of midshipmen at Annapolis from 1870–
1873. During the Civil War, Major General Carter organized
Union troops for Tennessee.

231 (a) In 1924, Duke (1856–1925) signed the Duke Indenture for a
$40 million endowment meant expressly to benefit hospitals,
orphanages, colleges and the Methodist Church in the Caro-
linas, and to create Duke University as a memorial to his

industrialist father. (The university's name was changed from Trinity.)

232 (a) The American Colonization Society, founded in 1816 by the Reverend Robert Finley of New Jersey, persuaded Congress to lend aid for land purchases. In all, about fifteen thousand blacks (freed by slaveholders or born to free parents) moved to the colony, which came to be called Liberia. The capital, Monrovia, was named for President James Monroe.

233 (c) White people, until John Quincy Adams's administration, were sold as indentured servants to be given their liberty after a specified time period. When he was fourteen, our seventeenth president (1808–1875), was indentured to a tailor. Eventually Johnson set up his own tailor shop, in Greeneville, Tennessee, and became celebrated for the quality of his hand. He continued to make his own clothes when he was president. Our thirteenth president, Millard Fillmore (1800–1874), was also an indentured servant, to a clothmaker.

234 (d) Her twenty-minute "act" toured the country—she needed the money for living expenses. The rising curtain showed a drawing room with a garden seen through French windows. Mendelssohn's "Spring Song" would be heard and Miss Keller's companion came on stage and told a little about Miss Keller's life. And then Miss Keller herself appeared and spoke for a few minutes. "Helen Keller has conquered again," The *New York Times* reported, "and the Monday afternoon audience at the Palace, one of the most critical and cynical in the world, was hers." Miss Keller said that the cause of the blind and the deaf was helped by her success. (Though blind and deaf from the age of nineteen months—as the result of an attack of scarlet fever—she had been graduated with top honors by Radcliffe, and would have married if her mother had permitted it.)

235 (b) And they were published without a by-line. After the reclusive Emily died, her sister Lavinia discovered Emily's haunting poems (one thousand of them) tied together with string in a dresser drawer and tried to interest publishers. One finally agreed to publish them on the condition that Lavinia pay for the cost. A definitive edition of Emily Dickinson's work was not published until the 1950s.

219

236 (d) High Street, near William Shakespeare's residence, was home for Katherine Rogers, who married Robert Harvard in 1605. Their son John (1607–1638) founded Harvard in 1636. During the college's first decades, the principal course of study was Hebrew—most of the students were preparing for the ministry and had to be able to read the Bible in its "original" language.

237 (a) The Know-Nothing party, which opposed the influence of foreigners, especially Catholics, stole the pope's gift. The public was shocked and contributions for Maryland marble slowed. Congress offered financial assistance, but Know-Nothings broke into the office of the Washington National Monument Society, which had been formed as the fund-raiser in 1833, and claimed the monument. In 1876 President Ulysses S. Grant approved a federal act that would complete construction. The new marble was of a slightly different color than that which the monument was begun—the two-toned appearance testifies even to this day to its shady history. (The cornerstone-laying ceremony on July 4, 1850, led to President Zachary Taylor's death a few days later. Sixty-five-year-old Old Rough and Ready overexposed himself to the heat, ate iced food that disagreed with him and developed fatal acute gastroenteritis.)

238 (c) Nellie Tayloe Ross succeeded her husband, William B. Ross, who had died midway through his term as governor of Wyoming. A month later she was elected in her own right but lost in a reelection bid in 1926. Mrs. Ross became a vice-chairman of the Democratic National Committee and the first woman (1933) to be director of the U. S. Mint; she was appointed by President Franklin Roosevelt. She died in Washington, D.C., on December 19, 1977, at the age of 101.

239 (c) About 7.1 gallons of absolute alcohol were consumed per capita per year.

240 (c) He turned his hand for a time to gentleman farming at Mount Vernon.

241 (a) General McClellan (1826–1885) was fired as commander of the Union army and ran unsuccessfully against President Lincoln in 1864. Bryan (1860—1925) ran three times: in 1896, 1900, 1904.

242 (d) Crane was a journalist in the Spanish-American War, then retreated to England, and then to Germany, dying in the Black Forest in 1900.

243 (b) The teaching of German was forbidden during the war, and it never regained its popularity.

244 (c) The nativists fought "foreign" influences and tried to uphold the "American" view. In secret rites, members would reply "I know nothing" when questioned, hence the party name. Some politicians believed that the bigotry of the Protestant Know-Nothings—they particularly resented German and Irish Catholics—might unite Americans and cause them to forget the slavery issue. The party disintegrated with the advent of the Civil War.

245 (d) Central Park—smack in the middle of Manhattan—was once, a century ago, 840 marshy acres littered with filth and shanties.

246 (c) The literary historian saw democratic idealism as the characteristic American idea.

247 (c) George Washington, Martin Van Buren, Andrew Jackson, Zachary Taylor, Millard Fillmore, Abraham Lincoln, Andrew Johnson, Grover Cleveland and Harry S. Truman.

248 (a) Douglass, fearing retribution when Brown was captured, fled to the British Isles, arousing much sentiment there against slavery in the United States. (Two of his sons fought with the Union army.)

249 (b) Because the "go-aheaditiveness" advocate desperately wanted to read "what sort of lines" were going to be written about him in the *Evening Sun*, the newspaper obliged with a four-column account. The headline was "Great and Only Barnum. He Wanted to Read His Obituary; Here It Is."

250 (a) A. I. Root, a beekeeper in Medina, Ohio, read a scanty report about the Wrights in a Dayton (Ohio) newspaper and realized its significance. His write-up was rejected by *Scientific American*, which as late as 1906 was asking its readers, "If such sensational and tremendously important experiments are being conducted in a not very remote part of the country, on a subject in which almost everybody feels the most profound interest, is it possible to believe that the enterprising American reporter, who, it is well known, comes down the chimney when the door is locked in his face—even if he has to scale a fifteen-story skyscraper to do so—would not have ascertained all about them and published them long long ago?"

251 (c) Eli Whitney (1765–1825) agreed to deliver ten thousand muskets in two years, but he didn't deliver even one for nearly three years. In producing the muskets, Whitney struck on one of technology's greatest advances—the concept of interchangeable parts. Any stock, for example, could now fit any barrel.

252 (c) The Wobblies (IWW for Industrial Workers of the World, formed in 1905) made an indelible mark on the history of American labor with their pamphlets, songs and poems as well as with their free-speech fights and strikes.

253 (c) Woodrow Wilson.

254 (b) 1845.

255 (c) She remained in detention on North Brother Island, in New York, until her death at the age of about 68 in 1938. She had worked as a cook in many homes and was herself immune from the carrier-borne disease.

256 (a) Alexander Hamilton Stephens (1812–1883) of Georgia, had served in Congress before the war. During the war the vice-president headed the Confederate delegation to the (unsuccessful) armistice conference with President Abraham Lincoln at Hampton Roads, Virginia. After the war he was imprisoned for several months in Boston, then was elected (1866) to the Senate but was refused his seat. In 1872 he was allowed to take his elected seat in the House. He was subsequently elected governor of Georgia.

257 (c) Without authorization they ended up buying half a billion acres of wilderness at less than three cents an acre—the Louisiana Purchase—which is larger than the combined areas of Portugal, Spain, Italy, Germany and France.

258 (c) A vigilance committee, consisting of men of Virginia City and Bannack, finally hanged him.

259 (a) They all first occurred during John Tyler's Administration (1841–1845). William Henry Harrison died after only one month in office, March 4-April 4, 1841.

260 (b) He later decided that the figure was "much too low."

261 (d) In February 1861 Lincoln offered to give up the fort if the Virginia convention, then considering secession, would adjourn *sine die*. On March 5 he learned that the Confederates had cut off food supplies from the fort, which soon would be forced to surrender. On April 6 he notified the governor of South Carolina that he would be sending a relief expedition to Sumter—provisions only, no munitions, and that resistance to the mission would be met with force. The Civil War started on April 12.

262 (c) Sullivan (1856–1924) combined the disciplines of the artist, the engineer and the visionary. His triumphs and despairs reflected the vicissitudes of the rising democracy that he strove to express. Function and quality were indeed a proud and soaring thing. He believed that art is expressive of the life of the people who produce it. He was to suffer from democracy's Achilles heel: the mediocrity of the men in charge, the distressing tendency of commercial-"democratic" society to reduce things to the lowest common denominator. He refused to compromise on design features and, of course, lost clients. And so there was a declining business and there were drink and a divorce. Inscribed on Sullivan's tomb by Chicago builders and architects: ". . . his drawings unsurpassed in originality and beauty; his writings rich in poetry and prophecy; his teachings persuasive and eloquent; his philosophy where, in 'Form Follows Function,' he summed up all truth in Art, Sullivan has earned his place as one of the greatest architectural forces in America."

263 (a) Bell (1847–1922) was on the East Coast, and Watson, who indeed heard the call, was on the West Coast, three thousand miles away. (The German Reis had invented the electric telephone, in 1860, but Bell is given credit for commercial success of the medium.) Thirty-six years later on a November afternoon in 1951 the Atlantic and Pacific Oceans were seen simultaneously on television for the first time, on the Murrow-Friendly debut edition of "See It Now": "It occurred to us that, until the electronics of television, no man had ever been capable of gazing at both oceans at the same instant. We thought that a medium capable of doing this was capable of providing reporters with an entirely new weapon in journalism."

264 (d) Asked if he thought that Adam was to blame for the failure of capitalism, the muckraking journalist-author (1866–1936) responded, "No, it was the apple." In *The Shame of the Cities*, which documented municipal corruption, he wrote, "The corruption that shocks us in public affairs we practice in our private concerns. There is no essential difference between the pull that gets your wife into society or for your book a favorable review, and that which gets a heeler into office, a thief out of jail, and a rich man's son on the board of directors of a corporation; none between the corruption of a labor union, a bank and political machine. And it's all a moral weakness. The spirit of graft and of lawlessness is the American spirit."

265 (d) In 1867.

266 (b) Old Fuss and Feathers (1786–1866) was supreme army commander for a score of years, but his strategy for splitting the Confederacy was widely ridiculed, then adopted. Unlike other generals, he was not a successful candidate for the White House, losing out in 1852 to Franklin Pierce.

267 (c) President Taft (1857–1930) weighed about 350 pounds, and a special bathtub had to be installed for him in the White House. After the presidency, he wrote weighty tomes as chief justice of the Supreme Court.

268 (d) Henry Roth (1906–   ) wrote no other book.

269 (c) Simon Legree, the wicked slave driver, for example, was from Vermont. (Emphasis in Mrs. Stowe's book was on the evil social effects of slavery, e.g., the separation of black families.)

270 (c) The president was stricken in 1921, a year after he had run as the vice-presidential candidate on the losing Democratic ticket, and was never able to walk again. Support by the National Foundation led to discovery by the immunologist Jonas Salk (1914–   ) of the vaccine that has helped to eradicate the disease throughout the world. More than fifty thousand Americans had been struck by polio in 1952, the year before Salk announced successful experiments with the vaccine.

271 (c) He composed much music, including "Melody in A Major," a semiclassical tune that became a popular ballad, then the rock 'n' roll hit. Dawes (1865–1951) was president of the German reparations committee, an ambassador to Great Britain, a delegate to the London Naval Conference, a winner of the Nobel Peace Prize (1925), president of the Reconstruction Finance Corporation as well as Calvin Coolidge's vice-president.

272 (a) In 1980 only 26.7 percent of the voting-age population cast its ballot for the winner, Ronald Reagan. In 1964 37.8 percent voted, and Lyndon B. Johnson won with 61.1 percent of the vote. Franklin Roosevelt netted 60.8 percent of the votes cast in 1936, but only 34.6 percent of the eligible men and women had cast their ballot. In 1836 only 11.4 percent of the voting-age population placed a president in the White House (Martin Van Buren).

273 (d) He did serve as an interim secretary of war for several months during the dispute over the Tenure of Office Act between the Congress and President Andrew Johnson. As president, Grant automatically became commander in chief of all the armed services.

274 (a) The Great Analyzer, by giving "a mighty impetus to the development of psychotherapy" in the United States, later confessed to Carl Jung, "I must admit that this has thrilled me more than anything else that has happened in the last few years." His lone visit to the States occurred in the same year, 1909, as did the visit by Bertha Pappenheim, known in the literature for more than fifty years as "Anna O.", the psychoanalysis' first patient. (In 1886 Freud had thought of moving to America to "find an existence" here if his two-month trial period in his new practice in Vienna didn't prove satisfactory, but "things went so well in Vienna that I decided to stay on, and [I was] married in the autumn of the same year." In 1920 Freud rejected an opportunity to lecture mornings at Columbia University and to treat private patients afternoons; he could make more money, he said, by working in Vienna.)

275 (a) Greenough (1805–1852) had been influenced by a replica of Phidias' rendition of the great half-nude seated Zeus grasping a spearlike scepter, and he wished his colossus, commissioned by the United States, to communicate the dignity of the ancient Greeks, those golden people. Instead, he suggested impropriety to those not acquainted with the classical style; it did not allow the public "to see the great man as their imagination had painted him." The statue proved to be too heavy for the floor and was immediately removed to the grounds outside, and then to the Smithsonian Institution, where it still sits. ("And who is that man without his clothes on, daddy?" "I cannot tell a lie, son. It's the father of our country.")

276 (b) Hale, in the guise of a Dutch schoolmaster rather than in uniform, had acquired intelligence on Long Island. It is believed that he was betrayed to the British by his Tory cousin, Samuel Hale.

277 (c) Edison patented "the Edison effect" but could think of no use for it, and he went on to other things. The Edison effect, it turns out, is the basis of the entire electronics industry. (Edison patented nearly thirteen hundred inventions; the phonograph was his favorite accomplishment.)

278 (c) In 1905 he loaded the world's strongest ship, the specially designed 184-foot-long *Roosevelt*, and headed north. For Peary also believed that "the true explorer does his work because the thing he has set himself to do is a part of his very being," and the Pole was, after all, a coveted goal still unattained by science. (If the Pole was not land but water, there would be nothing to claim—cold comfort indeed for Peary as he faced still another excruciating odyssey in snow, wind, ice and breath.)

279 (b) "I knew that none of these offers—motion pictures, lectures, writing 'my' story—could give me two things I wanted above all else: peace and emotional stability." Ignoring public acclaim, Scopes became a graduate student at the University of Chicago, a geologist for oil and gas companies, and converted to Roman Catholicism (in Venezuela) as a part of his commitment in marriage. Scopes renewed his friendship with Clarence Darrow, his attorney in Tennessee, in whose home in Chicago he and his wife were frequent dinner guests.

280 (a) Son of slaves, Mr. Young had amassed African and Afro-American literature during his travels throughout the United States.

281 (d) It had been an 8,578 word peroration. Forty-eight years later in 1889, there were torrential rains and strong winds during Benjamin Harrison's inauguration.

282 (c) Carnegie (1835–1919) was one of the first telegraph operators able to take messages by sound. After 1873 the rapid expansion of U.S. steel manufacturers became possible largely through his initiative.

283 (a) Commodore Decatur (1779–1820) had helped to court-martial Barron, a fellow officer whose promotion he had opposed.

284 (b) Hernando de Soto (C.1500–1542) had discovered the lower Mississippi in 1541.

285 (d) In May, 1804, the 40-odd party set out "under a jentle brease up the Missourie," and a year and a half later reached the Pacific in the Oregon country. Their return to St. Louis in September 1806, after having traveled 4,000 uncharted miles, was greeted with jubilation.

286 (d) The traitor's letter to George Washington was written in 1780 from the British warship *Vulture* after Arnold's flight from West Point. He died in London in 1801.

287 (b) Four were stoned to death by a mob of Confederate sympathizers a week after the besieged Sumter (not even one soldier was wounded there) had surrendered. The first soldier did not die in battle until mid-May. In four years about seven hundred thousand soldiers on both sides would be killed.

288 (b) "They knew they were pilgrims" first appeared in William Bradford's account of the Plymouth plantation.

289 (a) It was in 1830 after revelations which, he claimed, led him to the golden plates on which were printed the *Book of Mormon*. (The Indians, in Smith's translation were viewed as descendants of the lost tribes of Israel, and Smith and his followers undertook the task of conversion. The name of the Cherokee's one God happened to be Yehowa—so very close to the He-

227

brews' Jehovah; the Cherokee were of Iroquois stock, and the Iroquois lived in Smith's neighborhood.

290 (c) The Revolutionary War patriot, squire and transportation tycoon could not hold public office in his state of Maryland when he affixed to the Declaration "Charles Carroll of Carrollton" (referring to his community in Maryland) because he was a Roman Catholic; Roman Catholics in those days could not hold public office in the state nor could they be lawyers or teach the young. Carroll was the only Catholic to sign the Declaration.

291 (b) Public Enemy Number One (1899–1947) also said in the 1920s, "The American system of ours...gives each and every one of us a great opportunity if we only seize it with both hands and make the most of it.... We must keep America whole and safe and unspoiled."

292 (a) In 1855, a year before the thirteenth president (1800–1874) ran again for the office, this time as the candidate of the anti-Catholic, antiimmigrant Know-Nothing party. (On a visit to Rome, he had been presented to the pope. It was an ordeal for Fillmore, as he weighed the advantages against the disadvantages of publicity in the American press.)

293 (d) Wilbur, the older by four years, won the coin toss, but his try didn't work. Orville then tried—and took off for twelve historic seconds and 120 historic feet. In all, there were four successful flights that day—the longest was Wilbur's 851-foot, fifty-nine-second feat.

294 (d) His only elective office turned out to be the vice-presidency. He automatically succeeded the assassinated president, James A. Garfield, in 1881 and served out the remaining forty-two months of the term, suffering Bright's disease and steadily declining health. A former collector of the Port of New York, he did not actively support civil-service reform but signed the law setting up a Civil Service Commission. He signed measures excluding Chinese and regulating other immigration, after securing technical improvements in the legislation. A year after leaving office, Arthur died of a massive cerebral hemorrhage. (Woodrow Wilson was elected president twenty-two months after first holding public office, the governorship of New Jersey.)

295 (a) The French balloonist Jean-Pierre Blanchard, a French aeronaut who spoke little English, carried the president's letter from lift-off in a prison yard in the then United States capital of Philadelphia to the landing in Gloucester County, forty-six miles away in New Jersey in 1793. It was the first balloon ascension in the Western Hemisphere. Benjamin Franklin's illegitimate son, William, nine years earlier had written the first air-mail message, ballooned from Dover to Calais, noting, "I dare say, you will like to be one of the first who gets a letter across the British Channel by this kind of aerial conveyance."

296 (c) Essentially a practical chemist, Carver (c.1864–1943) was born of slave parents and was illiterate until he was almost twenty years old. He developed more than a hundred different products from the peanut and the sweet potato; the famous Carver's Hybrid was a cross between the short-stalk and tall-stalk cotton.

297 (d) At President James Monroe's request, Marie Joseph Paul Yves Roch Gilbert du Motier de Lafayette returned to the United States in 1824 for a hero's welcome and triumphant tour—though the French statesman feared that no one would recall who he was and what he had done. How wrong he was! Lafayette (1757–1834), who had encouraged French aid to the revolutionists and fought with Washington at Valley Forge and Yorktown nearly half a century earlier, was universally welcomed. In New Orleans he was literally a show-stopper; a performance in a theater there halted when Lafayette entered, and the audience rose as one in elation. Congress voted him a gift of $200,000 and a township of land. Earth from Bunker Hill was used to cover his grave in Picpus Cemetery in Paris. (After taking part in the American Revolution, Lafayette played a key role in the French Revolution. His reception in America was a pleasant surprise to the Liberals in France, who were encouraged and strengthened by it.)

298 (b) The Ohio newspaper editor and senator (1865–1923) was nominated and in 1920 elected by a large margin to be the twenty-eighth president. But a year earlier, the married Mr. Harding's long-time mistress, Nan Britton, had given birth secretly to their daughter, Elizabeth Ann Christian. The Hardings, by the by, were the only president and first lady to die during the term for which he had been elected. President Harding died in San Francisco in 1923 under circumstances that are still not completely clear; Mrs. Harding died in late 1924.

299 (a) The poet (1869–1935) was three times a winner of the Pulitzer Prize. Isadora's two children, by different liaisons (but not by Robinson), were killed in an automobile accident in 1913, and in 1927 she herself was accidentally strangled by a long scarf that had become caught in a wheel of the Bugatti in which she was riding.

300 (d) *Ben-Hur: A Tale of the Christ* was the first work of fiction to be blessed by a pope. (President Garfield (1831–1881) also liked to attend lectures by Charles Dickens, who paid a call on the White House in 1841 when John Tyler (1790–1862) was president. In *American Notes*, Dickens wrote that "We entered a large hall, and having twice or thrice rung a bell which nobody answered, walked without further ceremony through the rooms on the ground floor, as diverse other gentlemen (mostly with their hats on and their hands in their pockets) were doing very leisurely . . . A few were closely eyeing the movables, as if to make quite sure that the President (who was far from popular) had not made away with any of the furniture or sold the fixtures for his private benefit."

301 (c) Senators, members of the president's cabinet, clerks from government bureaus, porters, janitors, icemen, salesmen and office workers—an audience of 75,000—were present to register their indignation at the flagrant act of discrimination, and millions more listened to the radio broadcast. The concert was called by some "the greatest single event in the slow march of the American Negro to full equality as a citizen."

302 (a) The death of Dr. Lazear (1866–1900) was proof of the mosquito-transmission theory, and it indeed led to the effective control of yellow fever.

303 (c) The social reformer often criticized President Abraham Lincoln's handling of the Civil War. He succeeded Garrison as president of the American Anti-Slavery Society, championed labor and railed at academic conservatives.

304 (c) Fearing defeat by the Democratic nominee, General McClellan, in the forthcoming election, the Republican convention stampeded at the last minute. There was falsification of delegations by a clique of New England "copperhead" delegates, who wished to oppose Lincoln's leadership in any way they could. Knowing they could not succeed in removing Lincoln himself from the ticket, they chose to undermine his strength by nominating for vice-president former Senator Andrew Johnson, a war Democrat and military governor of Tennessee, a border state. Lincoln was bitterly disappointed, for he wanted Hamlin at his side again. Immediately after his reelection, the president offered Hamlin a cabinet post in the new administration, but the assassination interceded and Hamlin was to join the faction demanding President Andrew Johnson's impeachment three years later. As a Maine senator again, he espoused the cause of Chinese workers ("the yellow peril" to many) in railway construction in the West and championed civil rights for blacks—their education must be guaranteed so they could fully participate in the social and political growth of the nation.

305 (c) Fear of being charged with having monarchic pretensions, ambassadors being considered a device of monarchies, caused all presidents until Grover Cleveland to have the nation represented through ministries, or consulates.

306 (c) Jacob Coxey ran for president on the Farmer-Labor ticket in both 1932 and 1936. He died in 1951 at the age of ninety-seven.

307 (b) In 1789, his very first year as our very first president. One hundred seventy-three years later, President John F. Kennedy initiated direct government involvement.

308 (c) As sheriff of the Erie County jail in Buffalo, he was responsible (in 1871–1872) for the hanging of two murderers; one had stabbed his mother to death; the other, a gambler, had shot another man during a card game. Cleveland had also helped edit a book about cattle and had been a teacher in a school for the blind, mayor of Buffalo and governor of New York.

231

309 (b) John A. Tyler (the tenth president), Millard Fillmore (the thirteenth), Franklin Pierce (the fourteenth), Andrew Johnson (the seventeenth) and Chester A. Arthur (the twenty-first).

310 (d) Louis Philippe (1773–1850) had deserted the army of the French Revolution. He lived in exile for a score of years, then returned to France when the Bourbons were restored to the throne. He was king from 1830 to 1848.

311 (c) The Tory Benjamin Thompson (1753–1814) served as a lieutenant colonel in the king's forces. Later, the elector of Bavaria appointed him to high civilian and military positions to train Bavarian troops; and in 1791 Thompson was made a count in the Holy Roman Empire. From exile in England, where he was known as Count Rumford, he attempted in old age a reconciliation with his native land. He left most of his estate to the United States and endowed a professorship in applied science at Harvard.

312 (c) Governor Brandon of Alabama began every roll call with the cry "Al-a-bam-ah-h-h-h casts twen-ty fo-ah votes for Os-ch Double-yuh Un-n-n-der-r-r-wood!" and so impressive was his two-week performance that a New York radio station offered him a $10,000-a-year announcer's job. Mr. Davis (1873–1955) was a Wall Street lawyer and a former diplomat. He waged a losing campaign against President Calvin Coolidge, one of whose "cool" slogans was Coolidge or Chaos. He appeared before the Supreme Court in some 140 cases. His last major engagement was his defense of the physicist J. Robert Oppenheimer against charges that he was a security risk.

313 (c) The author was John Cotton, a Puritan preacher. The book was printed in Cambridge, Massachussetts, in 1646.

314 (d) The aggressive, controversial Dr. Walker (1824–1860) tried to set up a military empire built on slave labor, and his position as dictator was even officially recognized by President Franklin Pierce, in 1855. Five years later, after other adventures, he was captured by a British naval officer, turned over to Honduran authorities and executed by a firing squad.

315 (a) "West Virginia," the thirty-fifth state, broke away from Virginia over political and economic differences—one of three ways in which the boundaries of the thirteen original states were significantly different in 1776 from what they are today. Maryland then included the territory now making up the District of Columbia. (The District was ceded in 1801 to the federal government to serve as the site of the capital.) Massachusetts then included what is now the state of Maine. Maine became a state in 1820.

316 (c) Second in his class (1846) at West Point, McClellan (1826–1885) during the Civil War had come into possession of a copy of Robert E. Lee's orders but did not press his knowledge, nor did he pursue the retreating Confederate general. (He served as governor of New Jersey from 1878 to 1881.)

317 (d) The anthropologist (1901–1978) used to wake up at night "with the dreadful thought that the last man on Rarotonga might be dying this very minute." She was affiliated for forty-seven years with the American Museum of Natural History and was a curator there for five years. Miss Mead believed that "fathers are spending too much time taking care of babies. No other civilization ever let responsible and important men spend their time in this way. . . . Until about ten or fifteen years ago, most Americans were appallingly poor lovers. Then they began reading about it and things changed."

318 (a) Ladd, a sea captain, founded the American Peace Society in 1828.

319 (d) In 1956 the ex-president (1874–1964) told the fiftieth-anniversary celebration of the Boys Club of America that "a boy had two jobs. One is just being a boy. The other is growing up to be a man."

320 (a) The third president (1743–1826) had his by-line on only one book, answers to a set of twenty-three questions about the American continent, *Notes on the State of Virginia*. That Jefferson had written one of the world's most famous documents was not generally known for eight years after the Declaration of Independence had been promulgated. He said that there wasn't a new idea in the historic document—the object was not to be original but to declare what people already believed.

321 (b) Two weeks after the war had ended in 1815, and more than a month before news of the war's end even reached Louisiana. Because communications in those days were so slow, the United States declared war on Great Britain in 1812 because it did not know that British orders interfering with U.S. commerce had been repealed. Five days after the Battle of Lexington had ignited the American Revolution, it was learned—too late!—that Parliament had voted to allow the colonies to tax themselves and to provide for their own civil administration and defense. It took half a year for word to reach Washington that John Augustus Sutter and James Marshall had discovered gold in California in 1848, which is why it is known as the gold rush of '49.

322 (b) The former professor of vocal physics at Boston University moved swiftly from one interest to the other—eugenics, aviation, science, solar power and so on—but his principal concern was always the teaching of the deaf.

323 (a) The artist, Emanuel Leutze (1816–1868), had returned to his native country to study art in Düsseldorf. The painting, made in 1850 at the request of Congress, is false in almost every historical detail; the flag, for instance, was not adopted until after the event. Congress didn't like the painting, so Leutze gave it to the Metropolitan Museum of Art, in New York, where it is a popular attraction.

324 (c) The twenty-seventh president (1856–1924) said that the Constitution would suffer, that free speech and perhaps even the right of assembly would be hard-pressed. He went on to draft the Covenant of the League of Nations, to which the United States then did not subscribe.

325 (b) They all first occurred during Franklin Pierce's administration (1853–1857).

326 (c) The operation was performed by surgeons on a yacht cruising New York's East River during the president's second term; not even Vice-President Thomas A. Hendricks knew about it. The event wasn't made public until Cleveland died more than a decade later.

327 **(a)** With a cavalry escort, the Great Emancipator rode in a carriage through Richmond, surveying some of the 700 burned dwellings and stores and thousands of homeless whites and blacks. Six days later, on April 9, 1865, the South surrendered at Appomatox. Five days after that, the president was dead, the victim of a crazed Southern sympathizer's point-blank bullet.

328 **(a)** Eleven years after starting his automobile business, Ford established the consumer-commodity economy. Later he declared that the "real progress of our company" dated from that gesture. Ford, deeply committed to the idea of progress, established the eight-hour work day and introduced the practice of community services. He considered plants, workers and car-buyers as an organic whole—each element "ecologically" dependent on the other like so many cogs in a wheel. As long as the consumer society continued to grow, all would be well.

329 **(c)** Franklin (1706–1790) made the first pair of bifocal spectacles, invented the rocking chair, and was the first (1769) to charter systematically an ocean current (the "river in the ocean," the Gulf Stream), learn that a rough sea could be calmed by pouring oil on it, and start a foreign-language newspaper in the colonies (the German *Philadelphia Zeitung*, in 1732). His invention of the lightning rod (1753) was the first practical victory of science over a natural phenomenon.

330 **(c)** The widow of the Great Emancipator was treated in a sanitarium and improved to the point that another court in 1876 reversed the insanity verdict.

331 **(a)** Garfield (1831–1881) had been nominated for the presidency in 1880 on the thirty-sixth ballot, and won the campaign with a plurality of 9,464 votes out of a total of almost 9,000,000 cast. He was assassinated several months after being sworn.

332 **(b)** The ever-popular Thomas Riley Marshall (1854–1925) was Woodrow Wilson's veep (1912–1920). Later John Nance Garner served two terms as Franklin Roosevelt's vice-president and Richard M. Nixon served two terms as Dwight Eisenhower's. Spiro Agnew was reelected as Richard Nixon's vice-president. The last vice-president before Mr. Marshall to have succeeded himself is the only veep besides Mr. Agnew to have resigned—John C. Calhoun. Vice-President Marshall also once said, "The Vice-President of the United States is like a man in a cataleptic state: he cannot speak; he cannot move; he suffers no pain; and yet he is perfectly conscious of everything that is going on about him.

333 (d) The Irish-born Lyon (1750–1822) represented Vermont and Kentucky in the House. Later, when he was appointed an Indian agent to the Cherokee by President James Monroe, he moved to Arkansas and became a territorial representative to Congress. Another Irish immigrant, James Shields (1810–1879), was an Illinois senator for six years, a Minnesota senator for one year and a Missouri senator for thirty-one days. (Lyon was once involved in a violent cane and tongs fight in the House over a slur on his military record with the Continental Army. He is said to have dissuaded Andrew Jackson from taking part in the ill-conceived, ill-fated Burr Conspiracy to take over New York State and New England and create a separate nation.)

334 (b) He thought that Harriet Beecher Stowe's "runaway" best-seller had not gone far enough, though it stirred sympathy for the abolitionist cause and President Lincoln was to call it the ignition for the Civil War. (Rhetorically, Garrison was to ask why Negroes should bear their captivity with humility in a country that was supposedly founded on the right of free men to overthrow tyranny? "Talk not to them of peacefully submitting to chains and stripes—it is base servility! Talk not of servants being obedient to their masters—let the blood of the tyrants flow! How is this to be explained or reconciled? Is there one law of submission and nonresistance for the black man and another law of rebellion and conflict for the white man? When it is the whites who are trodden in the dust, does Christ justify them in taking up arms to vindicate their rights? And when it is the blacks who are thus treated, does Christ require them to be patient, harmless, long-suffering, and forgiving? And are there two Christs?")

335 (b) The widely read, syndicated political columnist (1889–1971), who twice won the Pulitzer Prize, did not once in the 1930s write a word about what the Nazis were doing to the Jews.

(Mr. Lippmann was also Jewish, a fact that he tended to keep a secret.)

336 (a) For years, Oliver Evans (1755–1819) had been petitioning state legislatures for patent protection: "Your petitioner hath invented an entire new plan of applying said powers to propelling land carriages to travel with heavie burdens up and down hills without the aid of animal fource with such velocity as may be convenient, and be guided by a person sitting therein secure from the clemency of the weather." Commissioned by the Philadelphia Board of Health to build a dredge for the docks, he adapted one of his steam engines and mounted it on a small barge. But how to move the dredge to the river? He built a truck with four wheels on which he mounted the dredge and then linked the steam engine by gears to drive the wheels. He named the contraption Orukter Amphibolos, "amphibious digger," and drove it through the streets of the city and to the docks.

337 (c) In the face of the Constitutional guarantee of freedom of the press, the *News* was suspended for eighteen months. The *World*'s editors were arrested on Lincoln's personal orders. (In May 1864 the Lincoln administration was embarrassed to learn that two newspapers in New York had published a proclamation "by the President" calling on the Union to observe a day of national fasting and prayer because the war was not going well in Virginia. It turned out that the *New York World* and *New York Journal of Commerce* had been "had" by a reporter, Joseph Howard, of the *New York Times* [which didn't publish the proclamation, which he had passed off as a dispatch of the Associated Press]. The erring newspapers were suppressed for a time by the government.)

338 (c) Stevens's life-long principle was Equality of Man before his Creator.

339 (d) Texts of this beloved art combine the word chase and literary pleasure. (The crossword puzzle as it is known today was first published in 1913 under the title "Word-Cross," in the *New York Sunday World*—it was diamond-shaped with no black squares.)

237

340 (c) Senator Logan (1826–1886) was a general in the Civil War, thrice a president of the Grand Army of the Republic, which he had helped to organize, and the defeated Republican vice-presidential candidate on James G. Blaine's ticket in 1884.

341 (a) After being censured, the Wisconsin Senator (and former tail-gunner in a dive-bomber) retreated to his room, watched soap operas on television and stared into the fire, and eventually became an acute alcoholic.

342 (c) The polymath (he could speak twenty languages) was a man for all seasons, preaching the symbiotic relationship of nature and human beings. He could always see the trees for the forest. "Man has too long forgotten that the earth was given to him for usufruct alone, not for consumption, still less for profligate waste.... There are parts of Asia Minor, of Northern Africa, of Greece, and even of Alpine Europe, where the operation of causes set in action by man has brought the face of the earth to a desolation almost as complete as that of the moon.... the earth is fast becoming an unfit home for its noblest inhabitant, and another era of equal human crime and human improvidence... would reduce it to such a condition of impoverished productiveness, of shattered surface, of climatic excess, as to threaten to deprivation, barbarism, and perhaps even the extinction of the species.... the multiplying population, the impoverished resources of the globe, demand new triumphs of mind over matter." Marsh (1801–1882) badly damaged his eyesight in childhood by reading an entire encyclopedia. He was graduated in 1820 from Dartmouth College and had a brief teaching career before studying law and joining the bar. He served seven years in Congress, condemning what he called "the criminal nature" of the Mexican-American War and vigorously protesting the extension of slavery. He saw the Civil War as inevitable; the Union was a geographical unit and could not be divided successfully.

343 (c) The authors of the *Communist Manifesto*, Marx and Frederick Engels wrote about 500 articles for the *Tribune* from October 1851 to March 1862—350 by Marx, 125 by Engels, about 12 jointly. The tone and theme of the articles did not adhere to a preconceived ideological line, common among their followers. Marx and Engels did try, subtly, to oppose *Tribune* policy, but found themselves many times in accord. Marx knew that he could not expect his articles to convert many Americans to his cause. He set about only to show social and political realities as he saw them. He had intellectual thoroughness and never wrote until he had fully researched the topic, exercising his talent for sifting much material and recognizing the significant.

344 (a) The Constitutional purpose of the census has not changed since the very first one: to provide the basis for fair apportionment among the states of seats in the House of Representatives. The first census covered the sixteen states and the Southwestern Territory, and there were five questions: Number of free white males sixteen years of age and older? Number of free white males under sixteen years? Number of free white females? Number of other free persons? Number of slaves? The first census, completed on August 1, 1790, placed the population at 3,929,625, which included 19 percent blacks (697,624 slaves, 59,557 free). The most populous state was Virginia, at 747,610, and the largest city was Philadelphia, 42,444. Massachusetts was the only one of the thirteen states to report no slaves. By 1800, the population had grown to 5,308,483. Scientific census-taking began in 1850, when the individual became the unit of study.

345 (b) The general's expertly crafted hairy-paw furniture probably was made in the early 1770s by one of Philadelphia's top cabinetmakers, Benjamin Randolph or Thomas Affleck, or even by both of them. The paws are of a shaggy Shetland sheepdog. (The British originated the hairy-paw style.) In 1982 a hairy-paw chair, even though it was downright ugly, was sold for $275,000 making it the most expensive chair ever auctioned. (General Cadwalader shot General Thomas Conway in the face during a duel that Cadwalader had called when Conway was agitating to remove General George Washington from Valley Forge.)

346 (c) He wrote fifty-two books in all, including novels, but none gained the fame of his *Spoon River Anthology*; when he died, it had gone into more than seventy printings. (As a lawyer, he represented the Hearst newspaper in Chicago, and defended a waitresses' union without a fee.)

347 (d) In 1871. (Forty-three years earlier, the distinguished President John Quincy Adams was charged with squandering federal money by installing a billiard table in the White House for gambling purposes.)

348 (a) Abraham Lincoln.

349 (a) In 1712, after slaves had killed nine whites in New York, eighteen slaves were burned to death, hanged in chains or committed suicide. After another riot in New York in 1741, fourteen slaves were burned to death, eighteen hanged and seventy-one deported. In the early 1800s, slaves' heads were placed on pikes along the Mississippi River. Between 1889 and 1922, there were at least 3,436 lynchings of blacks *and* whites. (At the end of the First World War, at least twenty-eight people were burned to death by mobs around the country.) In 1933, the first year of the New Deal, at least 42 persons were lynched.

350 (a) Masterson (1853–1921) was renowned for his reportage of boxing, and he was the model for "Sky" Masterson in the Damon Runyon story "The Idyll of Miss Sarah Brown," which became the brilliant musical *Guys and Dolls*.

351 (d) Addressing himself to the question "Is the airplane coming?" Dr. Newcomb said, "If I should answer not, I should be at once charged with setting limits to the powers of invention, and have held before my eyes, as a warning example, the names of more than one philosopher who had declared things impossible, which were afterward brought to pass. Instead of answering yes or no, I shall ask the reader to bear with me. . . . No builder of air castles for the amusement and benefit of humanity could have failed to include a flying-machine among the productions of his imagination. The desire to fly like a bird is inborn in our race, and we can no more be expected to abandon the idea than the ancient mathematician could have been expected to give up the problem of squaring the circle. . . . As the case stands, the first successful flyer will be the handiwork of a watchmaker and will carry nothing heavier than an insect. . . . The example of the bird does not prove that man can fly. . . . Imagine the proud possessor of the aeroplane darting through the air at a speed of several hundred feet per second!

240

It is the speed alone that sustains him. How is he ever going to stop?" On learning two years later that the Wrights *had* flown, Professor Newcomb said that it would be impossible for an aeroplane to carry passengers.

352 (b) Congress confirmed the commission, but did not give Lafayette troops to command. After Lafayette (1757–1834) was wounded in the Battle of Brandywine and distinguished himself at the Battle of Gloucester, he was given command of a division by General George Washington, and again he distinguished himself. He returned from a trip to France in time to participate in the capture of the British army at Yorktown, the last major battle of the Revolutionary War.

353 (c) Hobart (1844–1899) died prematurely of an illness officially described as "embarrassed respiration"—he literally ate himself to death—and so Theodore Roosevelt replaced him as President William McKinley's running mate in the 1900 national election.

354 (a) Illuminating-gas stocks fell on the stock markets of New York and London when the fecund Edison announced in 1878 that he would try to invent an electric light bulb.

355 (c) Salaries were so much in arrears that the legislators sometimes lived by borrowing money. In Philadelphia a mob of soldiers, having received no wages for six years, threatened to imprison the lawmakers until their arrears were paid. Congress kept one gallop ahead of its creditors, moving from Philadelphia to Princeton to Annapolis to Trenton to New York, and finally to Washington, D.C.

356 (b) The New England essayist and poet (1803–1882), who was the central figure of the new transcendentalist spirit, also noted that "the human body is the magazine of inventions, the patent-office, where are the models from which every hint was taken. All the tools and engines on earth are only extensions of its limbs and senses."

357 (d) Hill was executed by firing squad in Utah after being tried and found guilty of murder there. Many people believe to this day that the Swedish-American radical (and folk-song writer) was framed.

241

358 (d) Carl Sandburg (1878–1967), who told this story in a "See It Now" telecast with Edward R. Murrow, described President Lincoln as "a mountain in grandeur of soul. He was a sea in deep undervoice of mystic loneliness. He was a star in steadfast purity of purpose and service. He abides."

359 (c) The future president (1874–1904) had worked for twenty years as a mining engineer. He was in China during the Boxer Uprising at the turn of the century and was the American food administrator providing relief for starving civilians in Europe. The young Franklin D. Roosevelt said of Hoover, "He is certainly a wonder, and I wish we could make him president of the United States. There couldn't be a better one." Seven months before Wall Street laid an egg, the thirty-first president said at his inaugural, "Ours is a land filled with millions of happy homes, blessed with comfort and opportunity. I have no fear for the future of our country. It is bright with hope." Five days before the stock market crashed, Mr. Hoover said, "The fundamental business of the country, that is, the production and distribution of commodities, is on a sound and prosperous basis."

360 (d) The commander of the proslavery Confederate armies believed that "slavery is a moral and political evil in any society, a greater evil to the white man than to the black," and he freed his own slaves.

361 (a) Presidents John Adams, Thomas Jefferson, John Quincy Adams, Martin Van Buren, William Henry Harrison, Zachary Taylor, Millard Fillmore and James Garfield. The first president to veto more than 100 bills was "the Veto President," Grover Cleveland, who vetoed 584. The only four-time president, Franklin D. Roosevelt, is the champion, with 631 vetoes, of which only 9 were then enacted into law by Congress. (Congress did not override a Presidential veto until 1845, when the issue was payment for naval vessels ordered by President John Tyler.)

362 (c) He—General George C. Marshall (1880–1959)—was chosen over the heads of several senior officers and became the chief of army activities through the Second World War. As President Harry S. Truman's secretary of state, he proposed the European

Recovery Program—the Marshall Plan—which earned him the Nobel Peace Prize.

363 (c) The blind and deaf Miss Keller (1880–1968), whose books were burned by the Nazis in 1933, also said, "It has been a happy life. My limitations never make me sad. Perhaps there is just a touch of yearning at times. But it is vague, like a breeze among flowers. Then, as the wind passes, and the flowers are content... I can see a God-made world, not a man-made world."

364 (a) He declined both the commission offered by the Khedive of Egypt and an appointment by President Ulysses S. Grant as marshal of Virginia and instead worked as an insurance company agent. The general (1825–1875) had graduated last in his West Point class (1846), as did Lieutenant Colonel George Armstrong Custer in 1861.

365 (a) The Boston Brahmin (1850–1924) had little sympathy for progressive reform legislation, and led the opposition to President Harding's proposal that the United States join the World Court.

366 (a) Commander Matthew Fontaine Maury (1806–1873), a Virginian, had accompanied Marquis de Lafayette back to France in 1825. An accident then rendered him unfit for sea duty, and he wrote tomes on the physical geography of the sea and its meteorology. During the Civil War, he secured a number of English warships for the Confederate fleet and was in charge of coast, harbor and river defenses. After Appomattox he tried to establish a colony of Virginians in Mexico. (Another commander in the United States Navy, before Fort Sumter, was captain of the Confederate's *Alabama*. Raphael Semmes (1809–1877) directed the sinking or capture of more than sixty Union ships—he sailed around the world hunting for them.

367 (b) They all were candidates for selection by the electoral college to be the first president of the United States. Jay had been a commander of a colonial militia in New York; Harrison, a member of George Washington's staff during the war; Clinton, a brigadier general in the Continental Army; and Lincoln, a commander of militia in Massachusetts. The fifth candidate

243

was the electors' unanimous choice: Lt. Gen. George Washington, probably the best-known American of the day.

368 (b) The president pro tem of the Senate may have been president for one day in 1849. The inauguration of Zachary Taylor was scheduled for March 4, but it was a Sunday, and Taylor elected to take the oath of office on the following day. Many felt that Atchison, by virtue of senatorial position, had therefore been president for one day, but James K. Polk, who was leaving office, constitutionally probably still held the position for that extra day. (In the late 1850s, Atchison [1807–1886] returned to Missouri and conducted "border ruffian" raids into Kansas.) The date of a U.S. presidential inauguration has fallen on a Sunday five times in history, and the public ceremonies on each occasion were switched to Monday. The most recent such occasion was in 1957, the beginning of Dwight Eisenhower's second term. The constitutional requirement was met when Ike took the oath of office in a private ceremony in the White House on the Sunday; he then repeated the ceremony publicly on the Capitol steps the next day. In 1985, January 20 again falls on a Sunday—but it is the Sunday of Super Bowl XIX—the presidential inauguration will surely be moved to the following Monday again.

369 (b) Brown (1800–1859) settled his family in a black community that had been established at North Elba, New York, by Gerrit Smith. Captured after he and his band of twenty-one followers had seized the arsenal at Harpers Ferry, Virginia, Brown refused to plead insanity (for which there was considerable evidence); he was convicted of murder, promoting slave insurrection and treason against Virginia. He told the court: "I am yet too young to understand that God is any respecter of persons. I believe that to have interfered as I have done—as I have always freely admitted I have done—in behalf of His despised poor, was not wrong but right. Now if it is deemed necessary that I should forfeit my life for the furtherance of the ends of justice and mingle my blood further with the blood of my children and with the blood of millions in this slave country whose rights are disregarded by wicked, cruel, and unjust enactments—I submit; so let it be done!" "John Brown's Body" became an enormously popular song during the Civil

War among the Unionists, who saw Brown as a martyr; his actions, however, did little to mollify an outraged South, where he was seen as devil incarnate.

370 (c) Drake (1819–1880), who had been a railroad conductor, lost his money in a stock deal. (John Sutter [1803–1880], who found gold in California, lost all of his money, and John Charles Fremont [1813–1890]—"The Pathfinder," who had explored the Oregon Trail—lost a $10-million mining fortune.)

371 (b) It was in 1906, after yellow fever had been licked in the Canal Zone. The twenty-fifth president was also the first president to ride in an automobile, fly in an airplane or dive into the sea in a submarine. "You must remember," a British diplomat sighed, "that the president is about six." The Rough Rider (1858–1919) also wrote forty books, and left politics for almost two years in bereavement when his mother and his first wife died on the same day in 1884.

372 (d) Eighty-six changes were made in the Declaration between Thomas Jefferson's first draft and the document read out in public on July 4, 1776. The final version on parchment was not ready for signing for another two months; and the names of all the signators were not made public until the following January.

373 (a) His mother used to send little notes about Douglas to his teacher, usually requesting favored treatment.

374 (a) Tennessee in 1920 became the thirty-sixth, and last necessary, state to vote for the amendment: "The rights of citizens of the United States to vote shall not be denied or abridged by the United States or by any state on account of sex."

375 (c) President Dwight D. Eisenhower's aide (1888–1959) advocated active opposition to Soviet policy and liberation of "captive" nations under Soviet sway.

376 (b) George Washington, Andrew Jackson, William Henry Harrison, Zachary Taylor, Ulysses S. Grant and Dwight D. Eisenhower. Five other professional soldiers have been nominated for the presidency: Benjamin Lincoln, Winfield Scott, John Fremont, George McClellan and Winfield Scott Hancock. Only five presidents have served in the navy, and curiously, they were the presidents from 1960 to 1980: John F. Kennedy, Lyndon B. Johnson, Richard M. Nixon, Gerald R. Ford and Jimmy Carter. Mr. Carter was the only president to have been graduated from the Naval Academy. Zachary Taylor (1784 – 1850), a professional soldier for forty years, said, "I look upon war at all times, and under all circumstances, as a national calamity, to be avoided if compatible with national honor."

377 (a) *Charlotte Temple*, published in 1791, was a melodramatic work with wooden characters and a hackneyed plot—and it went through two hundred editions.

378 (c) According to the 1860 census. (The house butler, for instance, might himself be a free black but he would own his wife and *his* servants.)

379 (a) The young British officer would hang because British authorities had refused to relinquish the real murderer, who remained in protective custody behind their lines in New York. At the last minute—"a wonderful interposition of Providence," intercession by the foreign minister of France—saved Charles Asgill's life (in 1782), and he sailed back to Europe.

380 (b) All three services had been abolished quickly. The former colonists simply wanted nothing to do any longer with standing armed forces.

381 (b) At Tuskegee Institute in 1905, in the first year of his only full four-year term.

382 (c) At his inauguration as president of the Confederate States of America on February 18, 1861, Davis also said that the South wished to be free to consolidate and to gain international recognition. Five months from the end of the war, Davis argued that forty thousand slaves be hired to fight with the army, then let go after the war, which, presumably, the South would have won. (Davis was once married to the daughter of a president. A graduate of West Point [1828], he participated in the closing scenes of the Black Hawk War, then resigned his commission in the army [1835] and married Knox Taylor, daughter of Colonel Zachary Taylor, who fourteen years later became the twelfth president. Mrs. Davis died of malaria three months after the wedding. Davis became a recluse for eight years, then remarried, was elected to Congress, fought with Mississippi volunteers under his former father-in-law in the Mexican War, was elected to the Senate, and served the fourteenth president, Franklin Pierce, as secretary of war.)

383 (c) International recognition of the Wrights' feat didn't come until 1908 when there were demonstrations in France and at Fort Meyer, Virginia, before thousand of spectators. At Le Mans, Wilbur Wright flew for 113 minutes. At Fort Meyer, Orville Wright flew for 62 minutes and Wilbur flew for nearly 56 minutes with a journalist as a passenger. (It was at Fort Meyer, on September 17, 1908, that the first airplane fatality occurred. Orville was the pilot when a propellor blade broke and the craft fell one hundred fifty feet to the ground, injuring Wright seriously and killing his passenger, Lt. Thomas W. Selfridge, of the United States Signal Corps.)

384 (c) On March 15, 1913, about ten days after Wilson had become the twenty-seventh president.

385 (c) "My father had shouted and shot at the two white men who had set the fire and were running away," the black political and religious militant (1925–1965) remembered. "Our home was burning down around us. We were lunging and bumping and tumbling all over each other trying to escape. My mother, with the baby in her arms, just made it into the yard before the house crashed in, showering sparks. I remember we were outside in the night in our underwear, crying and yelling our heads off. The white police and firemen came and stood around watching as the house burned down to the ground."—Lansing, Michigan, 1929. Malcolm X (born Malcolm Little) was assassinated in Harlem.

386 (d) A couple of years after leaving office, General Grant (1822–1885) made a six-week visit in 1879 and told the ruling regent of the Manchu Court that "any course short of national humiliation or national destruction is better than war." On his return to the United States, the former chief executive made an unsuccessful bid for a third term. His memoirs, written as he was dying of cancer of the throat, were published by Mark Twain and brought wealth to the author's family and of course,

247

to the publisher. Richard Nixon (1913–   ) became the first president still in office to visit both China and Russia.

387 **(c)** In this celebrated freedom-of-the-press case in the mid-1730s, the editor's lawyers successfully contended that statements about New York Governor William Cosby, a Crown official, were true and therefore not libelous. When Zenger died, his wife became editor of the *Journal*. (A substantial proportion of the printers and newspaper publishers in colonial America were women. Six served as official printers to provincial governments.)

388 **(c)** None of the four candidates for vice-president under the eighth president, Martin Van Buren, received a majority of the electoral vote, so the decision was up to the Senate, and it chose Richard Mentor Johnson (1780–1850), a Kentucky representative and senator who had successfully advocated the abolition of imprisonment for debt and reportedly had killed the Shawnee chief Tecumseh, who was fighting with the British at Thames, in Ontario, in 1813.

389 **(b)** The eleventh president (1795–1849), the "Napoleon of the stump," a Tennessee congressman for seven consecutive terms, had been a "dark horse" selection at the Democratic convention in May 1844. He also kept four other campaign promises: the acquisition of California from Mexico; the settlement of the Oregon dispute; the lowering of the tariff; and establishment of the sub-Treasury.

390 **(b)** An easygoing freshman congressman, William Pennington (1796–1862), of New Jersey, was finally selected. He had been elected governor of New Jersey six times, though he boasted that he knew nothing of importance about the law.

391 **(b)** So sure was the Ohio senator (1800–1878) that President Andrew Johnson would be convicted—the pro tempore of the Senate, he voted against Johnson—that he began selection of his cabinet while the trial was in progress. President Johnson remained chief executive by the margin of one vote, and Wade was bitterly disappointed.

392 **(b)** After the War, Revere (1735–1818) turned out silverware that was among the finest in the colonial and post-Revolutionary periods and is highly prized today. He also worked with Robert Fulton in developing copper boilers for steamboats.

393 (a) The count was ordered by the thirty-third president, Dwight D. Eisenhower (1890–1969).

394 (d) The Texas New Dealer (1868–1967) began March 4, 1933, as Speaker of the House. At noon, he was sworn as Franklin D. Roosevelt's first vice-president. Later in the day, he took his place on the Senate rostrum.

395 (d) Weaver (1907–   ) had served President John F. Kennedy as administrator of the Housing and Home Finance Agency, the highest post that a black American had held in the executive branch of the government, but the president could not get Congress (principally because of southern opposition) to create a Department of Housing and Urban Development (HUD) with a director of cabinet rank; J.F.K. planned to appoint Weaver to that post. President Kennedy's successor, Lyndon B. Johnson, was successful in setting up HUD with Mr. Weaver as secretary. (The first black to sit in the Senate was the Republican Hiram Revels (1822–1901), who was elected to fill the Mississippi seat of Jefferson Davis after the Civil War.)

396 (a) At his death in 1799, the former president owned thirty-three thousand acres of land in five states, the District of Columbia and the Northwest Territory.

397 (a) Clay's dead bull.

398 (c) Andrew Jackson (1767–1845) was president. (The financial panic in 1837 was precipitated when the charter of the Second Bank of the United States expired in 1836, the government's money was distributed among several state banks and only gold or silver was accepted as payment for public land.)

399 (a) Albert Bacon Fall (1861–1944) served nine months in jail for having received $300,000 in bribes in return for granting leases in naval oil reserve lands in California and Wyoming without competitive bidding. The "Teapot Dome" oil and political scandal of the early 1920s broke into the open when Harry Slattery, an attorney and a conservationist who had opposed the appointment of Mr. Fall, provided investigators with the tips that convicted the Secretary. The Democratic opposition to the President had been about to give up efforts to prove fraud in the leasing of the naval oil reserves when Mr. Slattery stepped forward.

400 (a) Annie's feats of marksmanship were truly incredible. She could split a playing card held edge-on and hit coins tossed into the air. As a teenager she bested vaudeville marksman Frank E. Butler. They eventually married and played the vaudeville and circus circuits together. Irving Berlin's musical about her, *Annie Get Your Gun*, was enormously successful.

401 (c) The Twentieth Amendment went into effect in October 1933: "The terms of the president and vice-president shall end at noon on the 20th day of January, and the terms of Senators and Representatives at noon on the 3d day of January, of the years in which such terms would have ended if this article had not been ratified, and the terms of their successors shall then begin."

402 (d) John Adams, the second president, lost his bid for reelection in 1800 because of repressive alien and sedition acts and tactless disregard of the democratic spirit of the time. Adams' son, John Quincy, was unable to unite the sectionalists, and there were lingering doubts about the veracity of his victory over Andrew Jackson in 1824. Jackson's hand-picked successor, Martin Van Buren, seemed snobbish to the populace, and the horrendous depression of 1837 stuck the president with the stigma of maladministration. When Millard Fillmore signed the Fugitive Slave Law, he also signed away any political power that he may have held in the North; he wasn't even nominated for president by the Whig Party in 1852, but he (unsuccessfully) ran in 1856 as the candidate of the pro-American, antiforeigner Know-Nothing Party. Andrew Johnson was not nominated by the Republicans for a full-term bid in 1868. Grover Cleveland, the first Democratic president since the Civil War, became the first Democratic president to lose a reelection bid; a hostile Republican Congress had crippled his reform efforts and, though Cleveland won the popular vote, he lost the more important electoral vote to President William Harrison's grandson, Benjamin, who in turn lost to Cleveland in the 1892 campaign. Harrison's passive administration had nearly caused war on trivial issues, such as control of the naval

250

base in the Samoan Islands. Theodore Roosevelt did not run in 1908 for a second full term, though he was sorely tempted, but he became dissatisfied in 1912 with *his* handpicked successor, William Howard Taft; so he ran again, but a poor third, behind Woodrow Wilson and Taft, as the Bull Moose candidate. Herbert Hoover's second presidential bid was turned aside by Franklin D. Roosevelt during the Great Depression. President Gerald R. Ford lost to Jimmy Carter in 1976 and President Carter lost to Ronald Reagan in 1980.

403 (b) Surrendering in 1783 at Annapolis the army commission that he had accepted from Congress eight years earlier. Less than six years later, on April 30, 1789, George Washington became the first president of the United States.

404 (b) Goethe.